TAR HEEL MADNESS

GOLDEN AGES
OF COLLEGE SPORTS

TAR HEEL MADNESS

Great Eras in North Carolina Basketball

WILTON SHARPE

CUMBERLAND HOUSE
NASHVILLE, TENNESSEE

TAR HEEL MADNESS
PUBLISHED BY CUMBERLAND HOUSE PUBLISHING, INC.
431 Harding Industrial Drive
Nashville, TN 37211-3160

Cover design: Gore Studio, Inc.
Text design: John Mitchell
Research/administrative assistant: Ariel Robinson

Library of Congress Cataloging-in-Publication Data

Sharpe, Wilton.
  Tar Heel madness : great eras in North Carolina basketball / Wilton
Sharpe.
     p. cm. — (Golden ages of college sports)
  Includes bibliographical references and index.
  ISBN-13: 978-1-58182-474-2 (pbk. : alk. paper)
  ISBN-10: 1-58182-474-2 (pbk. : alk. paper)
  1. North Carolina Tar Heels (Basketball team)—History. 2. University of
North Carolina at Chapel Hill—Basketball—History. I. Title. II. Series.
  GV885.43.U54S53 2005
  796.323'6309756565—dc22
                                                            2005030095

For Caroline,
thank you, my love, my partner.
Each day with you is such a blessing

and for Ariel,
your assistance has been invaluable
and is so truly appreciated

CONTENTS

INTRODUCTION

My first introduction to North Carolina basketball, so often the case in the middle 1950s, was through a magazine. In this instance, it was the *Sports Illustrated/ESPN the Magazine* of its day—*SPORT*. The publication was most noted for its eye-popping color photographs by the lens wizard of the era, Ozzie Sweet.

In one particular issue, I remember gazing upon a riveting full-page color photo of a handsome, black-haired basketball player kneeling on one knee on an empty court in his Tar Heel uniform. It was Lennie Rosenbluth. For a 12-year-old kid, that's all it took to begin following the exploits of a player, who soon became a hero. His team, as it turned out, was one to watch. The 1957 Tar Heels, led by soon-to-be National Player of the Year Rosenbluth, captured the school's first NCAA championship in a classic triple-overtime win over Kansas and its budding sophomore center, Wilt Chamberlain.

Tar Heel Madness is a tangible and somewhat nostalgic rendering of the fabled basketball program at North Carolina, as told by the players, coaches, assistants, opponents, fans, and members of the media. It's Rasheed to Rashad, Smith (Dean) to Smith (Kenny), Michael to Montross, May to McAdoo, and all the Tar Heels in between. It's humor and history, character and coaches, heroes and highlights. If Carolina blue courses through your veins, this book is for you.

It's all Tar Heel.

— W. S.

ORIGINS
OF BLUE

T he undisputed Rolls Royce of college basketball.

Art Chansky
author,
on the UNC program

I f we had 35 or 40 people out to see a game in those days, it was pretty good. There wasn't much enthusiasm for basketball then.

Roy McKnight

member of North Carolina's first intercollegiate basketball team in 1910, letter winner in 1911 and '12

O nce you get into that family at North Carolina, you're a part of the future and a part of the past.

Brad Daugherty

center (1983–86)

WHAT IS A TAR HEEL?

Nicknames are a colorful breed, often reflecting some special characteristic of a region or area in which a school or university is located. One of collegiate sports' more fascinating monikers belongs to the University of North Carolina.

According to one story, the name Tar Heels dates back to the Civil War, where it was said that the soldiers from the state of North Carolina were tough, persistent fighters, who dug in their heels in their battles against their enemy from the North.

In fact, it is the legendary Confederate general Robert E. Lee who is credited with having coined the phrase. In 1864, when he spotted a North Carolina contingent during a battle outside the town of Petersburg, Virginia, Lee reportedly remarked, "There they stand as if they have tar on their heels."

L ennie Rosenbluth's long-range bombs, Michael Jordan's aerial acrobatics, Antawn Jamison's low-post power—the roll call of great Tar Heels players winds through the decades like a river.

John Nichols

author

• • •

W e practiced outdoors at first because the director of old Bynum Gym didn't want his pretty floor messed up. But we finally went to the administration about it, and he was ordered to let us use the gymnasium.

Roy McKnight

There was hardly anything such as a jump ball. When two men got the ball, they struggled for it fiercely. I [was] flung across the gym by a bigger man many a time.

Roy McKnight

* * *

They had a kind of no-nonsense, team-oriented "we" mentality that I don't think any other coach had. There was a mystique to North Carolina that the other schools didn't have.

George Karl
guard (1971–73)/17-year NBA head coach with five teams

N orth Carolina basketball was great before they arrived, it was great before Coach Smith arrived, and it will be great long after I'm gone.

Bill Guthridge
head coach (1998–2000)/
assistant coach (1968–97),
on the departure of stars Vince Carter and
Antawn Jamison, both of whom opted to forgo
their remaining college eligibility at UNC and
enter the NBA draft in 1998

T he individual is asked to take a back seat to the team player. Entrepreneurs need not apply; North Carolina looks only for men that follow the company line.

Steve Holstrom
author

C arolina comebacks under Dean Smith actually became more prevalent as each new generation of players bought into the tradition.

Art Chansky

❋ ❋ ❋

O ne of Dean Smith's best known innovations was requiring a player who scored a basket to point to the player who had thrown him the pass that led to the hoop. "Thanking the passer" became a trademark of Carolina basketball, pleasing Smith, who often commented that while everyone was celebrating the player who scored, the player who threw the pass went virtually unnoticed.

Adam Lucas

author/columnist/publisher

'57 Final Four Is First
ACC Basketball
Televised to State

The first time basketball was televised to the State of North Carolina involving an ACC team was the 1957 NCAA Final Four from Kansas City, Missouri.

Local TV producer C. D. Chesley took a small production team to the event to telecast the NCAA semifinal between North Carolina and Michigan State back to Carolinians. The game, a triple-overtime thriller won by the Tar Heels, 74–70, was followed two days later with the telecast of the NCAA finals between UNC and Kansas.

Again, a triple-overtime nail-biter held viewers captive back in Carolina country. In the end, the Tar Heels fought off the Jayhawks and their great young center, Wilt Chamberlain, 54–53, to claim the school's first NCAA crown.

Soon thereafter, based on his triumph in Kansas City, Chesley began to successfully market the ACC Saturday afternoon game of the week.

O n par with the New York Yankees, the Boston Celtics, the Montreal Canadiens, Notre Dame football, and a very small handful of other teams, Carolina basketball stood above even these in terms of consistency. Not once after 1966 has Carolina had a subpar [i.e., losing] season or one even close to it.

David DeWitt

author/editor,
on North Carolina's near-impeccable overall
record. The morbid 2001–02 season, in which
the Heels went 8–20 under Matt Doherty,
was not in the equation at the time of the
above quote

D espite his heritage, Sean May is one of the few Tar Heels who understands much of the history behind the [UNC] program. He is prone to bring up great comebacks of the past when the team makes a run, and when asked which Carolina basketball alumnus he'd most like to meet, he doesn't mention Michael Jordan or James Worthy or Vince Carter. Instead he picks Lennie Rosenbluth, the National Player of the Year in 1957, who led the Heels to a national championship.

Adam Lucas

L arry Brown, Johnny Yokley, Bobby Lewis, Larry Miller, Dick Grubar, Eddie Fogler, Charlie Scott, Steve Previs, George Karl, Jimmy Black, and Kenny Smith all took turns running Four Corners with success over twenty years. But the spread offense was redefined by Phil Ford from 1975 to 1978 and continued to be associated with the All-American guard long after he graduated and moved on to pro basketball. Ultimately, as the biggest single reason for the implementation of the shot clock in 1986, Four Corners changed the rules of college basketball.

Art Chansky

on Dean Smith's legendary slowdown game

A s I get older, I am even prouder to be associated with Carolina basketball. To be a small part of such an envied program is a special feeling. To be able to say I spoke to Dean Smith today is like saying I spoke to the president.

Mitch Kupchak
forward/center (1973–76)

THE CAROLINA BLUE

*T*ime *and memory tend to be selective when the short list of so-called "greats" is called. Too often, the unnoted player with the heart of a warrior goes unrecognized, lost in the shadow of a Jordan, a Worthy, a Felton, or a McCants. Look beneath the sheen of the well-oiled machine, and you'll see the might of the worker bees. Without them the Carolina Blue could never have generated 15 ACC regular season crowns, 15 ACC Tournament titles, and five national championships.*

P layers often go unnoticed who really help a team. I'm talking about unsung people, those who play when first-stringers are injured.

Dean Smith

head coach (1962–97), assistant coach
(1959–61)

C arolina basketball became a family that transcended generations. From Doug Moe, Larry Brown, and Billy Cunningham to Larry Miller and Charlie Scott to Phil Ford and Bobby Jones to James Worthy, Sam Perkins, and Michael Jordan to Eric Montross and George Lynch to Vince Carter and Antawn Jamison, Carolina players shared a bond of understanding of what it meant to be part of something larger than themselves.

David DeWitt

The Tar Heels finished with a 23–3 record in 1940 and 19–9 in 1941. The star of these teams was George Glamack, otherwise know as "the Blind Bomber." A football injury had left Glamack partially blind, yet he was quite able to find the basket. Glamack averaged nearly 21 points a game in his senior year. Remarkably, when he finished college, the Blind Bomber was North Carolina's career scoring leader.

Ken Rappoport

author/journalist

FAST BREAK: *Glamack at one time held the all-time NCAA Tournament single-game scoring record of 31 points, totaled against Dartmouth in 1941.*

I never saw the basket, but I saw the backboard. It was so big and it was so white. I designed a Braille system by watching the black lines on the floor near the basket. I just got to my spot on the floor and shot from there. I took a long time to develop it, but I developed it.

George Glamack
center (1939–41),
on working with his sight handicap

He could shoot with either hand. He'd have his back to the basket and just pivot. He rolled out and shot . . . the hook shot. He had it down to perfection.

Lew Hayworth
Tar Heel player (1942–44),
on teammate George Glamack

A lways an actor on the court, Bones McKinney sparred lovingly with referees. When a foul was called on him, McKinney would animatedly "thank" the official. If the foul provoked animosity from the crowd, McKinney would walk over to the official and put his arm around his shoulder. "Don't mind that booing—we all make mistakes," McKinney would say. Often, he would check at the scorer's table after scoring a basket to make sure he was given credit for the shot.

Ken Rappoport

❈ ❈ ❈

I always enjoyed playing with him. He kept the team loose. He was also very witty, but he didn't clown around when he had to play basketball.

John "Hook" Dillon
forward (1945–48),
on teammate Bones McKinney

P ete Brennan is probably better remembered at North Carolina for a single shot he made against Michigan State in his junior year. . . . It was the national semifinals in 1957, and North Carolina trailed Michigan State, 64–62, with 11 seconds left in the first overtime period. It looked like it was all over for Carolina, but Spartan star Johnny Green, at the free throw line, missed the foul shot. Brennan snared the rebound and took off downcourt with the ball. Two Michigan State players were back to defend, so Brennan pulled up at the foul line and hit a jumper to send the game into a second overtime. The Tar Heels eventually won, 74–70, in triple overtime and then beat Kansas and Wilt Chamberlain for the national title in another triple-overtime dandy.

Ken Rappoport

I f fans were to argue Dean Smith's most important player during his tenure at North Carolina, one name that probably wouldn't arise is Rusty Clark. . . . The six-foot-ten Clark supplied the muscle from 1966–69 while playing on the first of Smith's great teams. Clark was not the team's best player; that honor was held by forward Larry Miller. However, Clark was the final piece of the puzzle, as the Tar Heels won their first ACC title since 1957 and posted an 81–15 record during his time there.

Ken Rappoport

H e was a lot like Joe Namath. When he made up his mind to do something, he would do it and do it well.

Dean Smith

on guard/forward Larry Miller (1966–68)

W hen Larry Miller started playing varsity ball at Carolina, the townspeople from his hometown of Catasauqua, Pa., a suburb of Allentown, scraped up $4,000 to get Tar Heel games broadcast on an Allentown radio station. It was money well spent. For three years, Miller was the primary player on Dean Smith's early great teams in the late sixties.

Ken Rappoport

N one of my close friends called me Charlie. Neither did my parents. It was like a stage name.

Charlie Scott
guard/forward (1968–70)

✦ ✦ ✦

I t was pretty bad. If our fans acted that way toward a visiting player, I would be ashamed. Playing basketball was the easy part.

Charlie Scott
on the racial harassment he received from opposing players and fans during road games

G eorge Karl's physical all-out style thrilled Tar Heel fans at North Carolina from 1971–73. Never one to worry about scrapes and bruises, Karl was constantly diving for loose balls, earning the nickname "the Kamikaze Kid."

Ken Rappoport

❖ ❖ ❖

I still get letters from Coach Smith. He's taken some clippings and circled the number of times I've used the word *I*. "Don't we mean 'we,' George?" I judge my year on how many times I hear from him on that.

George Karl
in 2001

T he greatest point guard in Tar Heel history? For Dean Smith, it was Phil Ford without question. But could Kenny Smith be far behind? Ford launched the point guard tradition at North Carolina when he came to Chapel Hill in 1974. Kenny Smith, among others, carried it on with style. He was named National Player of the Year by the *Basketball Times* in 1987. To be sure, there were other great Tar Heel point guards through the years. To name a few: Jimmy Black, Jeff Lebo, King Rice, Derrick Phelps, Jeff McInnis, and Ed Cota.

Ken Rappoport

U nquestionably, Dean Smith's favorite competitor on the [1985] team was Steve Hale, whose heart and hustle far surpassed his talent.

Art Chansky

A s a junior, the only year he made All-ACC [second team, 1988], Jeff Lebo set the UNC record for free-throw percentage until Shammond Williams broke it in 1998.

Art Chansky

FAST BREAK: Lebo closed his career in 1989 as UNC's all-time leader in three-point scoring.

Rick Fox, a handsome Bahamian, had taken up basketball late and defied all odds by playing two years at an Indiana high school and then winning a scholarship to Carolina. When he arrived in the United States from Nassau, almost the only thing he knew about American college basketball was what he had seen on a large-screen TV in the lobby of a resort hotel.

Art Chansky

on the Tar Heel forward who played from 1988 through '91

Across the U.S. and the world, there are lots of concert pianists who have never played the piano. Rick Fox was a basketball player who just had to start playing basketball.

Al Rhodes

Fox's Warsaw, Indiana, high school basketball coach

THE RECRUITMENT
OF THREE-YEAR-OLD
HUBERT DAVIS JR.

At this time we want to officially begin the recruitment of Hubert Jr.

— Bill Guthridge

(Said jokingly to Walter Davis's brother, Hubert, in 1973, referring to the latter's three-year-old son. Ironically, Hubert Davis Jr. would wind up at Chapel Hill [1989–92] and later star in the NBA.)

The talent pool, you say, must be pretty lean to have to dig down and begin recruiting a three-year-old. Well, like many lines of dynastic royalty throughout the centuries, consider the genetics.

Walter Davis, one of the heralded stars in Carolina history, is your uncle. And your dad, he's not exactly a chump on the hardwood himself. That's the world that little Hubert Davis Jr. was born into on May 17, 1970. As a teenager, Davis Jr. recalled a visit to his house by the immortal Dean Smith. Smith could be forgiven for thinking he'd walked into the den of a serial killer.

"He came to my house and came in my room and there were pictures of him all over my

walls," says Davis Jr. "He was like, 'Oh my gosh, who is this guy?' He said he didn't think I could play [at UNC]. I was a family friend, and he said he didn't want to see me sit on the bench all four years when I could go to a lower Division I school and play. But I was really persistent, and he said if I really wanted to come, I had to realize I wasn't going to play. I said fine, and the rest is history."

After one day of practice, one of the UNC assistants coaches was wide-eyed. "Hubert is a lot better than we thought."

Hubert Davis Jr.'s "history" included several Kodak moments, including his pass to Rick Fox for the historic game-winning bucket over top-ranked Oklahoma in the 1990 NCAA Tournament. He left Chapel Hill as the 15th-leading career scorer in Carolina history and the school's second-leading three-point scorer of all time. He is still the current record-holder in four three-point categories, including most three-pointers in a game (tied) and highest career three-point percentage.

Davis then went on to a 12-year NBA career with six teams, leading the league in three-point percentage (.491) with the Dallas Mavericks in 2000.

Even the Carolina coaching gods occasionally miss one.

He's one of the most underrated point guards ever to play basketball. It's a hell of a statement, but he didn't get the credit he deserved. Give Jimmy Black the ball, and you just had to run up the court. You knew it was going to get up court. You give Jimmy any defensive assignment, and he's going to lock the guy up, like the guy at Houston [Rob Williams]. He didn't score a field goal. Nobody talks about that. Jimmy was a great player, a great leader, and a lot of fun to be around.

Matt Doherty

forward (1981–84)/head coach (2001–2003)

I had confidence in Jimmy Black from day one. . . . I was sold on his savvy. We were looking for someone who could get people the ball.

Dean Smith

If I can just do my part to help us win, then that was important to me. I didn't do anything flashy. I didn't do anything that would make you say, "Man, he's a great player." But I thought I would do a lot of things to help win games. Instead of sprinting faster, I would run longer.

Jimmy Black
point guard (1979–82)

Being a role player is like dating your sister. There's nothing sexy to it, there's nothing exciting to it, but it was my role. Hey, I wasn't going to shoot the ball more than Michael Jordan or James Worthy or Sam Perkins. So I knew if I wanted to play, I had to do the little things. I enjoyed distributing the basketball. I enjoyed playing defense. I enjoyed winning.

Matt Doherty

O ne night Michael [Jordan] called me and said, "Hey, remember now, you told me you were going to Carolina," And I said, "I'm not going to let you down; we're going to room together." The whole time I was thinking, *Well, let's visit Kentucky.* I was impressed with their campus. Then one night I just woke up and said I'm going to Carolina. . . . And I kept my word to Michael.

Buzz Peterson
*guard/forward (1982–85),
member of the 1982
national championship team,
on his promise to Jordan when both were in
high school. Peterson, a highly recruited prep
star, met and befriended Jordan at one of the
many basketball camps attended by the
nation's top college prospects*

R anzino Smith wasn't supposed to be here but became an important player for us. He was an incredible threat, a dynamic shooter.

Rick Brewer

UNC sports information director emeritus, on the former Chapel Hill High School star who was considered only a marginal player when he initially arrived on campus. Smith would record nearly 41 percent of his three-point shots during his senior season (1988), while averaging 11.7 points per game

J awad Williams was the glue that was holding this team [2003–04] together. His quiet leadership became a constant during the turbulent 2002–03 season, and by the time the year ended Williams was publicly being compared to George Lynch, the revered senior leader of the national champion 1993 Tar Heels.

Adam Lucas

J awad Williams is an extremely coach-able player. During his freshmen year, [head coach Matt] Doherty and the staff worked with him to add a head fake to his post repertoire and then watched with surprise when he used it flawlessly in a game just days later.

Adam Lucas

M ore than anybody else on the team, Jackie Manuel has bought into what makes North Carolina's team do well. He's bought into all the little things. He's bought into complete intensity when he's out there. He's playing with a sense of urgency. . . . He tries to do everything he's asked to do. On the defensive end of the floor, even when he makes a mistake, it's because he is trying to do too much. It's never a failure of omission.

Roy Williams
head coach (2004–)

H is dedication to doing exactly what his coach asks of him endears him to Williams, who sees in Jackie Manuel what he wants to see in the rest of his players.

Adam Lucas

FAST BREAK: *When Roy Williams came back to Chapel Hill before the start of the 2003–2004 season, he presented Manuel with an option: play tough defense and shoot only when wide open or transfer out of UNC. The then-junior elected to stay and became a model of the prototypical selfless Williams team player.*

A cyclone of long arms and legs.

Adam Lucas
*on gangly guard/forward Jackie Manuel
(2002–05)*

Word from the annual summer pickup games is that rising sophomore forward David Noel appears ready to explode after a solid freshman campaign. Reports range from glowing to gushing about the Durham native, who would be an important piece of the puzzle for a team lacking frontcourt depth.

Adam Lucas

in 2003

I was a role player at North Carolina. *SportsCenter* didn't make players like me feel good, but Coach Smith did. We didn't make ESPN's highlight reel, but in our team meetings Coach Smith went out of his way to praise us for setting good screens, making good passes to the post, or helping teammates on defense. He recognized the little things we did to help the team.

Pat Sullivan
guard/forward (1991–93, '95)

F or every Bob McAdoo, the NBA Rookie of the Year and MVP, was a Dudley Bradley, who never scored in double figures. For every Mitch Kupchak, who continually overcame injuries to win an NBA title, was a Tom LaGarde, who never fully recovered from a blown knee his senior season to reach his pro potential. For every Walter Davis, another NBA Rookie of the Year and two-time all-star, was a Mike O'Koren, *USA Today*'s best all-around pro player who did not make an all-star team. For every Kenny Smith, who set NBA records for three-pointers, was a Joe Wolf, a career journeyman whose biggest claim to fame was lasting twelve years with seven different NBA teams. For every Hubert Davis, a great shooter who made it, was an Al Wood, a better shooter who didn't. And for every Rick Fox, who turned out to be a better pro than college player, was an Eric Montross or Jerry Stackhouse, who turned out worse.

Art Chansky

TAR HEEL
CHARACTER

E ach player must make a great effort to appear enthusiastic. By acting this way, the player will often become enthusiastic even if it was not his inclination when he first took the court.

Dean Smith

H e helped us to see life doesn't have to be a missed free throw.

Ron Green Sr.
*Charlotte Observer sportswriter,
on Bones McKinney*

Y ou know what you have to do. You have one shot. Go get it done.

Scott May
*1987 consensus All-America,
National Player of the Year at Indiana,
and father of Sean May,
to his son before the 2005 NCAA finals*

A lot of people talk about putting in a North Carolina system. There is no system. It's a philosophy on how to play the game: hard, smart, together.

Jeff Lebo
guard (1986–89)/Auburn head coach (2004–)

❀ ❀ ❀

People who have inner strength, inner affirmation, don't need the external affirmation associated with the winning team. Those who don't have that inner feeling depend on sports to give it to them. That, I think, is the wrong use of sports.

Dean Smith

❀ ❀ ❀

It's all about heart, you know. That's what our team has, we have heart.

Raymond Felton
point guard (2003–05)

I t was difficult for me to tell a student not to be politically active on his campus when I felt the chief reason why they were there was to ask questions and develop their own convictions.

Dean Smith

T he way I was taught, freedom is for everyone, not just for some.

Dean Smith
after accompanying a black student to a Chapel Hill restaurant in 1959. The student was served, and segregation eventually died out in the town

D ean has great character. He's an exemplar. He's all he appears to be. You never get Dean to talk about himself.

Christopher Fordham
former UNC chancellor

M y father said, "Value each human being." And we did.

Dean Smith

* * *

W e're human beings first, coaches and players second. In the sixties, we had to strike an extremely delicate balance between the two.

Dean Smith

* * *

I practiced like I played. So when I played, playing was fun. Practice is work. You're working on the idiosyncrasies of what your game needs, so when the game comes, you showcase it and you utilize it. You build your game on it. Practice wasn't just a place to take time off. You work on things in practice.

Michael Jordan

shooting guard (1982–84)

M y mom was my hero. I idolized her and how much she cared about her family. I don't think she knew it was the Golden Rule, but she always talked about treating people the way you'd want to be treated. She just thought it was the right thing to do.

Roy Williams

FAST BREAK: Williams's mother, Lallage, quit school after the tenth grade to work in a cotton mill and then a shirt factory for over twenty years to support her family. Often she worked 60-hour work weeks. When Roy was a teenager, she would come home from working all day at the shirt factory and start her second job—ironing clothes—for extra money.

A nytime a person does something hard, something which is difficult, there is a camaraderie which comes with the experience which is hard to achieve other places.

Dean Smith

T hose guys are my brothers out there and anybody who goes after my brother, I've got their back.

Sean May
center (2003–05),
after a play in a 2003 game against Davidson,
in which May got in the face of a Wildcats
player who had roughly fouled Rashad
McCants

T he disciplined person in society is the truly free person. We give our players discipline to make them free.

Dean Smith

C arolina really prepared me for some things I wasn't wise about and am still learning about. Those are things where you lay down the groundwork for life after basketball.

Sam Perkins
center (1981–84)

T his is the time when you guys become a good team. If you want to be a good team, this is where you prove it. You have to stay together and figure this thing out.

Roy Williams

to the 2004 team, his first at UNC, down two points to unranked Cleveland State with three minutes to play. The Tar Heels responded to Williams's challenge for an 82–76 victory

I f I'm going to play one minute, I'm going to play one minute hard.

Jim Braddock

guard (1980–83)

I t was the first time I had ever seen Coach Smith visibly upset, and I was shocked. But more than anything, I was proud of him.

Charlie Scott

North Carolina's first African-American basketball player,
after a game at South Carolina in which a courtside spectator yelled a racist remark at Scott, who was leaving the court following the game. Smith had to be restrained from going into the stands after the perpetrator

B ecause it was such a great example of perseverance, Woody Durham usually mentioned Carolina's spectacular come-back win over Duke in 1974 whenever he gave talks in high schools.

Ken Rappoport

FAST BREAK: *in that legendary 1974 Duke-UNC game, Duke was up, 86–78, with 17 seconds to play. The Tar Heels made a stunning comeback to tie it, before winning in overtime.*

S uccess is something that can over-whelm you. . . . If you go out and search for success, you never really get it. It's one of those things that you just go out, work hard, and try to achieve certain things; let things happen the way they are going to happen.

Michael Jordan

⚜ ⚜ ⚜

E nd-of-game situations never caught our Carolina teams by surprise because we prepared for them every day in practice. We knew what to do and when to do it, more by instinct than direction. Although we looked to Coach Smith for advice dur-ing games, we did not have to think, What do we do next? He had taught us what to do, when to do it, and how to execute in those crucial late-game situations.

Eric Montross
center (1991–94)

I really believe any leader must do what he says. I think that's extremely important to do what you say.

Dean Smith

Some have called me a pioneer. . . . I'll let others make that call. I do know that I was on the cusp of a changing society, and Coach Smith was great in helping me deal with a lot of issues. . . . If he believed something was morally right, he would stand up for it, and he didn't worry if it was popular or unpopular to do so.

Charlie Scott

When people say all these great things about us, it's us. So let's have the negative things be about us too.

Roy Williams

on his belief that a win is a team win and a loss is a team loss; that an outcome is never just about an individual's play, good or bad

I think he thinks his competitiveness is greater than mine, and I think mine is greater than his. But you know how it is, you can't correct someone who is older than you about something like that.

Rashad McCants

forward/guard (2003–05), commenting lightheartedly on both his and coach Roy Williams's contempt for losing

I told him the reason why we won this game is because he had heart and wouldn't let us fail. He carried us in the first half. . . . He was a totally different Jawad Williams from what I'd seen the last four games. He was the old Jawad Williams, dunking on people and making plays.

Sean May

on his teammate, whose hot hand kept North Carolina in the game during the first half of the Tar Heels' 2005 NCAA Final Four semifinal win over Michigan State. Williams totaled 20 points for the game

S ome years, I didn't think we'd make the Final Four, and we did. Some years we were knocked out in the first round when I thought we were the better team. Each time I felt, life goes on.

Dean Smith

W e've got to know that the name on the front of the jersey, North Carolina, is more important than the name on the back.

Roy Williams

THE LIGHTER SIDE OF BLUE

G o feel the bench.

Dean Smith
*to Mike O'Koren, who told Smith he was
"feeling it" in explanation of a bad shot taken*

I plead guilty to driving through life at about 80 miles an hour, drinking 60,000 Pepsi-Colas, smoking some two million cigarettes, and threatening the lives of several hundred referees.

Horace "Bones" McKinney

center (1946)/two-time ACC Coach of the Year at Wake Forest (1960, '61)/ABA Carolina Cougars head coach (1970, '71)

❋ ❋ ❋

I knew it was a dummy of me because of the long nose.

Dean Smith

on being burned in effigy by UNC students during his fourth year as head coach at North Carolina, following a 22-point loss to Wake Forest in 1965

❋ ❋ ❋

I can't. The rope's too tight around my neck.

Dean Smith

when students asked him to speak after a 1965 victory over Duke. Earlier that season, Smith had been hung in effigy after a loss to Wake Forest

H ow would I know if I was asleep?

Dean Smith
on former Tar Heel head coach Frank McGuire's story that Smith once sleepwalked while the two were roommates on the road

❊ ❊ ❊

I thought the man who invented basketball was Naismith, not Deansmith.

Bill Foster
former Duke coach

❊ ❊ ❊

H e said he saw a couple hippies on Main Street, and then he really felt better.

Dean Smith
on Charlie Scott's trip through downtown Chapel Hill before deciding to attend North Carolina. Scott would become the Tar Heels' first African-American player, in 1966

During preseason drills in 1961–1962, his first year as head coach, Dean Smith invented the "tired" signal. By raising a fist to the bench, any Tar Heel could take himself out of the game and then put himself back in by saying, "Coach, I'm ready." Not that the system was flawless. Smith still remembers with amusement that in the very first game of the season he forgot about the ploy. When Larry Brown gave him the "tired" signal running by the bench, Smith stood up, thrust a fist back at Brown and said, "Yeah, Larry, way to go!"

Art Chansky

I would have hit it if I'd tried. I was a punter in football.

Dean Smith

*denying that he tried to kick his chair and missed
when J. R. Reid once was called for a foul*

❀ ❀ ❀

It makes me sound like I'm bald.

Dean Smith

*on North Carolina's current basketball arena,
nicknamed "the Dean Dome"*

❀ ❀ ❀

We have barbers in Chapel Hill, too.

Dean Smith

*to Sam Perkins, late returning from a haircut
in Durham*

❀ ❀ ❀

When it reached the point where they said, "Pass the ball, sir," that was taking it too far.

Dean Smith

*on the decorum at the Air Force Academy,
where Smith was an assistant coach from
1956 through '58*

P laying at Myrtle Beach is unusual. We have a chance to lose a lot of money right there. I probably would've just told Raymond [Felton] that I would come and eat dinner at his momma and daddy's every time I go to the beach instead of taking a home game to Myrtle Beach.

Roy Williams

second-guessing himself and a tradition
he originated of occasionally scheduling
a North Carolina home game in the vicinity of
a player's hometown

FAST BREAK: *The game against UNC-Wilmington in Myrtle Beach, only an hour from point guard Felton's hometown of Latta, S.C., netted zero dollars for the North Carolina athletic department, whereas a typical Tar Heels home game in the Smith Center generally brings in a figure in the neighborhood of $350,000.*

A ll-American? You're not even All-Madison Square Garden.

Horace "Bones" McKinney

trash-talking to seven-foot center Bob Kurland, Oklahoma A&M's National Player of the Year, during the NCAA finals at the Garden in 1946. The Aggies won, 43–40

❊ ❊ ❊

H ere I am with a wife and a kid, and I'm smoking and hiding from a man just two years older than me.

Horace "Bones" McKinney

whose service stint during World War II left him, at 27, as a player nearly as old as then-UNC head coach Ben Carnevale in 1946

W ell, we reached the Final Five.

Dean Smith

*on losing to Arizona in the NCAA
West Regional Final in 1988*

❋ ❋ ❋

W e can play with anybody in the country. The trouble is there are 150 teams that can play with us.

Dean Smith

❋ ❋ ❋

T his is a women's soccer school. We're just trying to keep up with them.

Dean Smith

referring to another Tar Heels dynasty at UNC

L arry Brown has offered me a job as a janitor or something with the 76ers.

Dean Smith

on what lies ahead after retirement

◎ ❀ ❀

C an you imagine how many rocking chairs I'd get?

Dean Smith

on the wisdom of not announcing his retirement in advance

❀ ❀ ❀

T he Bobcats took UNC's Raymond Felton fifth. "He has a six-foot, four-inch wingspan," notes [TV analyst] Jay Bilas. Seriously? I always thought it looked like it was in the six-foot-three area. Thanks to ESPN's fun little draft-fact thingie, we just learned that Felton "writes poetry in his spare time." I think I would pay $7,500 to hear him recite Tyrone Green's "Kill My Landlord" to Stu Scott right now and pretend that he wrote it.

Bill Simmons

"Page Two," ESPN.com

T hey were so busy pointing at each
other after they scored, that we just
threw the ball downcourt and scored.

Len Elmore

Maryland star forward during the early 1970s,
on his team's taking advantage of Dean Smith's
policy of a scorer acknowledging an assist
by pointing to the particular player after
a UNC basket

K ing Rice is our Bush. I'd hate to have
to find out who our Quayle is.

Dean Smith

during a 1990 press conference, in which the
UNC coach alluded to his star point guard,
equating the team's lack of a quality backup at
the position to the similar disparity evident in the
offices of the presidency and vice presidency
in Washington

A w, shucks, you boys come over to the governor's mansion for supper anytime you want.

Luther Hodges

former (non-lettering) Tar Heel player in the late 1910s and onetime North Carolina governor (1954–60), to the national champion North Carolina Tar Heels, returning from their NCAA finals win over Kansas in 1957. The governor had been attempting to deliver a formal welcome-home speech, but the celebratory noise continually drowned him out. Throwing in the towel, Hodges instead offered the above words to the returnees

Y ou had to run the steps if you cursed. I had to run them a couple of times.

Michael Jordan

on the punishment meted out by Dean Smith for swearing

I thought it was a new necktie. I started to tie a knot in it but discovered it was a dead rattlesnake.

Steve Previs

Tar Heel player from 1970 through '72,
on one of the dead snakes that teammate
Dennis Wuycik would toss around the school
dormitories as a practical joke

❀ ❀ ❀

H aving Dean Smith ask to you redo the Carolina uniforms is like having God ask you to redo the uniforms for the archangels.

Alexander Julian

fashion designer and UNC graduate,
who revamped the Tar Heel uniforms that
debuted in the 1991–92 season

❀ ❀ ❀

I t's a great outfit to take on a date.

Hubert Davis Jr.

guard/forward (1989–92),
on Julian's abovementioned new-look uniforms
for North Carolina

H e swam more like a rock than a fish.

Buzz Peterson
*teammate (1982–85) and friend
of Michael Jordan,
on Jordan's less-than-athletic swimming
capabilities*

FAST BREAK: *Peterson once had to jump into a pool where Jordan was playing water polo to rescue his friend who had ventured too far into the deep end.*

❋ ❋ ❋

O ur problems have been with the guys in the blue shirts, not the striped shirts.

Jim Valvano
*late North Carolina State head coach
and TV color analyst,
commenting on a suspicion within the ACC
that Dean Smith intimidated young referees*

❋ ❋ ❋

T his'll really be big news back home, unless Dean Smith retires tomorrow.

Jim Valvano
*after N.C. State won the NCAA championship
in 1983*

I hope next time they throw dollar bills. That will get my attention.

Kenny Smith
point guard (1984–87),
on being hit by a penny while at the foul line
during a game at Marquette in the middle of
the 1985–86 season. The imperturbable
Smith went on to hit both shots for a 66–64
UNC win

Oh, gosh, I knew it was somewhere . . . because I got a wire from Billy Cunningham. I thought it had already happened.

Dean Smith
in answer to the question of how he felt as his
800th career win approached

It's amazing you can go from the West Coast to the East Coast in a matter of five minutes.

Vince Carter

guard/forward (1996–98),
on being picked No. 5 overall by Golden State
in the 1998 NBA draft, with teammate
Antawn Jamison selected No. 4 by Toronto.
The two teams then immediately swapped the
Tar Heel players in a trade

I kid Coach Smith and tell him he's the only man I know who has over 180 children and only four of them are girls.

Phil Ford

point guard (1975–78)/assistant coach
(1989–2000)

Did I mention that he could sometimes be as subtle as a train derailment?

Charlie McNairy

Tar Heel player from 1995 through '97,
on Dean Smith

How nice for the University of North Carolina to send a dean to talk to us!

Mother of Phil Ford

when informed by her husband and son that
Dean Smith was coming for a visit

HEROES
AND ICONS

A s soon as we had a lead, I knew there wasn't any way we could lose. He was our Goose Gossage.

Dean Smith
on point guard Phil Ford

FAST BREAK: *Gossage was a dominating nine-time all-star relief pitcher for the Chicago White Sox, New York Yankees, and San Diego Padres, among others.*

C art Carmichael could drive for the basket with unbelievable speed and hold himself in the air for a long time, like he was suspended.

Norman Shepard

head coach (1924),
on the first North Carolina athlete in history
to be named All-America in any sport.
Carmichael played from 1922 through the
1924 season

H e was the most graceful player you ever saw. Jack never threw the ball up there. He fully intended to make every shot.

Curtis "Sis" Perry

Tar Heel player in the early 1920s,
on "Mr. Basketball," Jack Cobb

The multitalented Jack Cobb could do it all: pass, defend, rebound, and run the floor. He was so versatile that fans immediately dubbed him "Mr. Basketball." Above all, Cobb could score. As the school's first three-time All-American, Cobb averaged 15 points a game—not bad even by today's standards, but extraordinary considering that his team averaged only 35 points a game. For his outstanding play, Cobb was named the National Player of the Year by the Helms Foundation in 1926.

John Nichols

At six foot two, Cobb was a skyscraper for his day, literally head and shoulders above the crowd. He was a ferocious rebounder, slick passer, and deadly shooter from his forward position.

Ken Rappoport

on the early Tar Heels star who played from 1924 through '26

O ne of the first stars of the "Carolina Pipeline" [from New York City] was Lennie Rosenbluth. A six-foot–five forward, Rosenbluth began his career at North Carolina in 1954, and from the moment he stepped onto the court, his game opened eyes across the nation.

John Nichols

FAST BREAK: The Carolina Pipeline came into existence during the coaching tenure of Frank McGuire, New York City born and raised, who tapped into the vast talent base on the city's playgrounds when he took over the Tar Heels coaching job in 1953. Refugees from the NYC-Chapel Hill Underground Railroad include: 1957 playmaker Tommy Kearns, three-time All-ACC guard York Larese, future coaching legend Larry Brown, and All-America guard Kenny Smith.

L ennie could just flat-out score. Long range, in the lane, open court—it didn't matter. He could fill it up.

Joe Quigg
center (1956–57),
on teammate Rosenbluth

N.C. STATE PASSES
ON ROSENBLUTH

Can older Carolina fans imagine the great Lennie Rosenbluth driving the lane and hitting a twisting off-balance shot for the Wolfpack on his way to becoming North Carolina State's season and career scoring average leader?

Had it not been for a teacher's strike in New York City during the early 1950s, Rosenbluth likely would have suited up in red and white rather than Carolina blue.

Harry Gotkin, a recruiter of New York City high school talent, alerted then-Wolfpack coach Everett Case about Rosenbluth, whom Gotkin believed Case might want. But due to a teacher's strike, much of the city's high school basketball had been shut down. As a result, Rosenbluth wasn't sharp in his workout and failed to impress Case, who passed on the young Bronx star.

Gotkin then contacted Frank McGuire, who would soon head up the North Carolina Tar Heels, and sold the New York-born-and-bred coach on Rosenbluth. The UNC record books and the fabulous 1957 season offer ample proof of Rosenbluth's star-studded path forged at Chapel Hill.

N icknamed "the Kangaroo Kid" for his sky-high leaping ability, Billy Cunningham averaged 23 points and 16 rebounds a game in 1962, sparking North Carolina to a 15–6 record.

John Nichols

T wenty-six of Dean Smith's players were selected in the first round of the NBA draft over thirty-seven years, from Billy Cunningham in 1965 through Vince Carter and Antawn Jamison in 1998.

Art Chansky

S ophomore Charlie Scott capped a 17-point comeback over unbeaten Utah in December of 1967 with the winning shot and, fifteen months later, scored 28 points in the second half against Duke to revive the Tar Heels in the ACC Tournament title game [won by UNC, 85–74].

Art Chansky

A Year at Chapel Hill

So great is the status of the North Carolina basketball program that even a player who spends only one year in Chapel Hill will always be associated with the Tar Heels.

The 2005 national champs boasted the best freshman in America and the second-best pro prospect (going by the NBA draft, where he was selected No. 2 by Atlanta), when Marvin Williams made his brief but impactful presence felt.

Another famous one-year-only star was 1972 forward Bob McAdoo, a junior college transfer who found himself in Carolina blue after UNC's commitment from high school player of the year Tom McMillen fell through at the last minute. At the time, Dean Smith had a no-JC policy in effect but made a timely concession with North Carolina native McAdoo. After a spectacular junior season, in which he averaged more than 10 rebounds and almost 20 points per game, McAdoo headed for an all-star career in the NBA.

The 6–9 McAdoo had earned a starting berth with his long arms and long-range shooting ability. Though his teammates were glad to have such a talent, the veterans were somewhat uncomfortable with—perhaps resentful of—McAdoo's instant emergence. *Sports Illustrated* even referred to him in a feature story as a "tall, dark stranger in the middle."

Art Chansky

Tar Heel basketball fans have a special connection with their point guards, beginning with the patron saint of the breed, Phil Ford, who remains the school's all-time scoring leader. Ford, a Rocky Mount, North Carolina native, was the first freshman ever to start his first collegiate game for Dean Smith.

Adam Lucas

P eople ask me why I play Phil Ford so much. Well, his cheerleading and jumping get in the way on the bench.

Dean Smith

on the zealous enthusiasm of his stellar four-year starting point guard. Ford was nicknamed "Bugs Bunny" by teammates for his animated emotionalism

P hil Ford not only became one of the best practitioners of the Four Corners offense, he was named to the All-America team three times and was named the player of the year.

Ken Rappoport

I t was the best four years of my life.

Phil Ford
on his UNC days

He was so good defensively. He was really good early, too. His freshman year, he was starting in the Final Four and he still got better. Big Sam was skilled and very smooth even at age 20. . . . He was a three-time All-American. He was the fourth pick in the draft.

Dean Smith

on Sam Perkins

James Worthy was the only high school recruit I was sure would be an outstanding college player.

Dean Smith

James Worthy's ability to score in clutch situations earned him the nickname "Big-Game James."

John Nichols

When we needed a bucket, we could just dump it down low to James and get out of his way.

Michael Jordan

on James Worthy

WORTHY COMES UP BIG
IN '82 NCAA FINALS

It was mano a mano, and Georgetown University's goliath center, Patrick Ewing, was setting the bar, logging 23 points, 11 rebounds, two blocked shots, and three steals, as the 1982 NCAA championship game against North Carolina wound down.

But the Tar Heels' James Worthy happened to be having a career day himself, ripping the nets for 28 points, dunking five times, and soon to figure in a bizarre play in the game's final, suspenseful moments.

Just 15 seconds remained, as Carolina, down by one, fed the ball to freshman Michael Jordan, open on the left wing. Jordan elevated for a jumper, letting fly a 16-footer and nailing a two that now put the Tar Heels up by a point.

With plenty of time for one last shot, the Hoyas brought the ball downcourt. But Georgetown guard Fred Brown, mistaking Worthy for a teammate, passed the ball directly to the surprised Carolina forward, who then dribbled out the clock.

Good fortune had smiled on Carolina. The Tar Heels, NCAA kings for the second time in their history, had just won Dean Smith's first national championship.

I thought James Worthy was a better college basketball player, but you go back and look at the tape at some of the things Michael [Jordan] did. He was the most competitive.

Woody Durham
longtime Tar Heel broadcaster

C oming out of high school, I had all the ability in the world, but I didn't know the game. Coach taught me the game— when to apply speed, how to use my quickness, when to use the first step or how to apply certain skills in certain situations. I gained all that knowledge so that when I got to the pros, it was just a matter of applying the information. Dean Smith gave me the knowledge to score 37 points a game, and that's something people don't understand.

James Worthy
forward (1980–82)

I f you told me when he first got here that Brad Daugherty would have been the first pick in the NBA draft, I would have laughed.

Dean Smith

on his star center from 1983–86. All-America as a senior and a five-time NBA all-star, Daugherty was the No. 1 selection in the 1986 NBA draft

H e's a greyhound. Not a shepherd, not a bit pull—a greyhound.

Al Menendez

*NBA scout,
on Kenny Smith*

B ecause of his basketball forte, flying dunks, and flat-top haircut, J. R. Reid got lots of attention.

Art Chansky

J unior center Pervis Ellison from Louisville was considered college basketball's premier man—but that was before J. R. Reid came along. Only a sophomore, Reid has established himself as college basketball's low-post land baron. He owns everything in the paint. He'd be a number-two lottery pick, or maybe even number one ahead of Danny Manning of Kansas.

Roy Johnson

Atlanta Journal-Constitution,
on the Tar Heel forward/center in 1988

H e should be carrying the bags of our seniors. I've never seen so much attention paid to someone who's only the third- or fourth-best player on his team.

Dean Smith

on freshman J. R. Reid's appearance on the March 2, 1987, cover of Sports Illustrated

He's had moments of being very, very good and moments of being very, very bad.

Dean Smith
on guard/forward Rick Fox (1988–91)

＊ ＊ ＊

He had more technicals than anybody else. . . . Each time, my rule, he sits down next to me for five minutes. And he learned, because then the team has to run sprints for him the next time out.

Dean Smith
on post player Rasheed Wallace (1994–95)

＊ ＊ ＊

I think Jerry Stackhouse is a natural leader, without doing a lot of talking. He's really a competitor inside, but you'd never know watching it from the outside.

Dean Smith

＊ ＊ ＊

Because of the above-the-rim playing style which he often employed, Jerry Stackhouse was continually being compared to Air Jordan during his time at Carolina.

Ken Rappoport

N o matter what happens to me in my career, one of the things I'll be most proud of is that I got to play for Coach Smith.

Antawn Jamison
forward (1996–98)

H e started to become a pure shooter halfway through his sophomore year. He became a better defensive player, because he had long arms and learned to move his feet. Of course, he is such a great athlete. The best jumper we had. He's going to continue to get better every year, you watch.

Dean Smith
on Vince Carter (1996–98)

That Rashad McCants would be a basketball prodigy seemed almost predetermined. Just weeks after he was born on September 25, 1984, his father James wrote in his son's baby book, "The next Michael Jordan."

Adam Lucas

❋ ❋ ❋

I've still got film footage of [him] flying over everybody. He took over the place. I told him right then, "No more playing with kids for you."

James McCants

father of Rashad, who pulled his son from recreation league basketball at age twelve and inserted him into men's competition. Author Adam Lucas described the young McCants's involvement in playing hoops with kids his own age as "the equivalent of Barry Bonds moonlighting in a church softball league"

Rashad McCants

R ashad McCants considered himself a player who thrived on emotion, a swashbuckling dueler who loved to feed off the crowd.

Adam Lucas

❀ ❀ ❀

I know I can be hard to be around some-times. But I want you all to know that I'm a good person. I'm a good kid.

Rashad McCants

to the audience at the team's annual award banquet, after being named the Tar Heels' MVP by coaches and teammates for the 2003–04 season

❀ ❀ ❀

R ashad McCants came into his own after New Year's '04, gunning more big shots than any Tar Heel in recent memory: Carolina's last 10 points to upset eventual '04 national champion Connecticut. A school-record-tying eight treys to sink Clemson. A series of daggers to sweep N.C. State.

Grant Wahl

Sports Illustrated

R ashad is such an offensive weapon that he's the guy the other coach talks about the most. He has an ability to score and make shots with people guarding him about as good as anybody I've ever had.

Roy Williams
on McCants

❋ ❋ ❋

I f McCants has a weakness, it's his 'tude, not his toughness.

Grant Wahl

❋ ❋ ❋

R aymond Felton is the "yes sir, no sir" man who must encounter difficulty on the court before he will show emotion. McCants, meanwhile, shows emotions as he gets off the bus.

Adam Lucas

P eople within the program promised Roy Williams that he had never had a point guard like Raymond Felton.

Adam Lucas

❋ ❋ ❋

T alcnt-wise, Raymond Felton is better than any point guard I've ever played with. He can go on the court and do anything.

Sean May

❋ ❋ ❋

I see things happening before they happen. I can get the ball on one end of the court and know something is happening at the other end. I pass the ball and all of a sudden, [a player] is there. It's just a sense I have. It's nothing I can explain or that anyone taught me.

Raymond Felton

❋ ❋ ❋

W hen I see Raymond Felton, I see one big heart.

Roy Williams

H e is that missing link, he makes this team. You take him out, and the pieces just fall apart. We need him at all times.

Sean May

on point guard Raymond Felton

M ost times, when someone has gotten that much hype before you see them play, it's kind of a letdown when you watch them for the first time. That's not a slap in the face, it's just reality. Very seldom does someone live up to those types of expectations. But the first time I saw Raymond [Felton] play, I was in awe. He is very talented for a young point guard.

Phil Ford

Raymond Felton

I hate to put this kind of pressure on Raymond, but he and Phil Ford are two of the finest college guards I've ever seen.

Dean Smith

I lways creative with the dish, he's harder to figure now that he's become more of a scorer.

ESPN the Magazine

on Raymond Felton,
ranked No. 4 nationally among college
basketball's 2004–05 best "Improv Artists"

I love playing for Carolina. This is the only school I wanted to play for.

Raymond Felton

He's the team MVP and the best player in the nation.

Sean May

on Raymond Felton

He's probably the closest thing that I've had to an indispensable player in 17 years as a head coach.

Roy Williams
on Raymond Felton

He just plays with a lot of passion and fire. He can't help but get it done.

Sean May
on talented freshman-turned-NBA second overall pick Marvin Williams

He's pure old school; no pretense, all power. Well, except for that nifty footwork and soft touch.

ESPN the Magazine
*on Sean May,
ranked No. 3 nationally among 2004–05
dominant inside men, "the Beasts Within"*

K ids, I want you to look at this guy. His dad was an All-American, but this guy will never be anything. His dad worked hard in practice every day, but this kid doesn't love the game of basketball. His dad worked harder in one practice than he has worked in his whole life. That's why he'll never amount to anything in basketball.

Bobby Knight

*to a group of summer basketball campers,
which included then-eighth-grader Sean May.
Knight was comparing the youngster to his
father, Scott May, whom Knight had coached
at Indiana*

W hen we'd play at the Y, I'd have to beg people to pick him. He was really bad. He couldn't shoot, he couldn't do anything.

Scott May Jr.

on younger brother Sean

Sean May

He's tough, he can score, he can defend. He's a big-time player.

Marvin Williams
forward (2005),
on teammate Sean May

● ● ●

He uses his body so well. He was almost unstoppable and played amazingly all over the floor.

Mike Wilkinson
Wisconsin forward,
on Sean May

FAST BREAK: *May dominated the matchup between he and the 6–8 Wilkinson in the 2005 NCAA Syracuse Regional Final, scoring 29 points, as UNC upended the Badgers, 88–82. May was named regional MVP.*

● ● ●

He's a beast. If we don't stop him in the first 10 seconds of a possession, it's over.

Bruce Weber
Illinois head coach,
critiquing film of Sean May, who tallied 22
points in the Tar Heels' 2005 Final Four
semifinal romp over the Illini, 87–71

LEGENDARY COACHES

T he unfortunate thing about national titles is no matter how good you are every year, they only equate one team as being the winner. As many big wins as Coach Smith had, as many great teams as he had, they will look at that [his two national championships] as his greatest accomplishment, but I don't. I can count a hundred unbelievable accomplishments on the court, and thousands off the court.

Billy Cunningham
*forward (1963–65)/four-time NBA All-Star
with Philadelphia/Philadelphia 76ers
head coach (1978–85)*

H e played basketball every day of his childhood and adolescent life—even in driving rain, the snows of New York winters, and the steaming heat of summer.

Anonymous acquaintance
of North Carolina head coach
Frank McGuire

on McGuire's formative years in New York City

I felt like I stuck out like a sore thumb.

Frank McGuire

head coach (1953–61),
on coming to Carolina country from the streets
of New York City

F rank McGuire replaced Tom Scott as coach at North Carolina. He was given one ultimatum: beat North Carolina State, which had won 14 straight games over the Tar Heels. McGuire did that in his first season. Then in 1957 he beat everybody.

Ken Rappoport

F rank McGuire, the irrepressible Irish carpetbagger from New York, captivated the media as well as the fans during his nine years in Chapel Hill, highlighted by his team's fairy-tale 1957 season of 32–0 and the national championship.

Art Chansky

❋ ❋ ❋

H e always coached from a confidence standpoint, telling a player, "What do you think I recruited you for?"

Dean Smith

*on mentor and UNC head coaching
predecessor Frank McGuire*

❋ ❋ ❋

I don't think it's fair to say he wouldn't play them unless they were from New York. That's true, but it's a terrible thing to say.

Dean Smith

*on McGuire's preference for players from his
familiar turf of New York City*

F rank McGuire left in the wake of a gambling scandal and NCAA recruiting violations, and Dean Smith took over as the Tar Heels' head basketball coach in 1961.

Ken Rappoport

❀ ❀ ❀

T he worst year of my life.

Frank McGuire

on the 1961 season, after which the North Carolina program went on NCAA probation for recruiting violations and involvement in a gambling scandal. McGuire chose not to ride out the turmoil and resigned, paving the way for Dean Smith's ascendancy to head coach

❀ ❀ ❀

H e played basketball at Kansas for the legendary coach Dr. Forrest "Phog" Allen, a spellbinding speaker who had a knack for inspiring his athletes.

John Kilgo

columnist/broadcaster/author, on Dean Smith's collegiate basketball career

W ith Smith on the team, Kansas won the national championship in 1952 by defeating St. John's, 80–63, and its nationally prominent Frank McGuire.

John Kilgo

FAST BREAK: *Seven years later, Smith would become McGuire's assistant coach at UNC.*

* * *

Y ou give the university a basketball program it can be proud of, and you'll have a job here as long as I am chancellor.

William Aycock

former UNC chancellor,
to young Tar Heel assistant Dean Smith, upon
elevating Smith to head coach following Frank
McGuire's resignation after the 1961 season

* * *

W e ask prospects, "What is your goal in college?" If their goal is to get an education and become a better player, we feel we have a chance to sign them. If they want to average thirty points as a freshman, we don't.

Dean Smith

There's something about the man that makes us work hard not to disappoint him.

Joe Brown
Tar Heel player from 1967 through '69,
on Dean Smith

❋ ❋ ❋

If there was an "innovation" at Carolina, it was to put our best ball handler in the middle, rather than a big man. Often the effect of the Four Corners was psychological, to show that we were in command. Of everything.

Dean Smith

❋ ❋ ❋

That's when I thought we would be okay. I had the loyalty of my players.

Dean Smith
on returning to Chapel Hill from a road loss in
January 1965 and spotting a dummy of
himself hung in effigy on the UNC campus.
Star forward Billy Cunningham yelled for the
bus to stop, before storming off and angrily
tearing the dummy down

I t didn't come to us all at once, but later we all wished we'd done what Billy C. did. It was the single most important thing emotionally I had ever seen.

Bob Bennett
guard (1964–66),
on Cunningham's previously mentioned
chivalrous act defending his coach's honor

A team is most dangerous the game after it has hit rock bottom.

Dean Smith

D ean Smith taught us that basketball games are won on the practice floor. Nobody could prepare a team like Dean. Nobody.

Billy Cunningham

Y ou watch a fellow like Dean Smith. If North Carolina loses, he's ready to play the next game. And in the meantime, he'll sleep at ease.

Frank McGuire

I think Dean Smith was as fine a teacher of the game as there has ever been. I think sometimes he taught too much. I believe in keeping things simple.

John Wooden
legendary UCLA coach (1948–75)

He can get angry. But he gets angry at the action, not the person. He won't hesitate to bounce some chalk off your head if you're going to sleep while watching game film.

Lee Dedmon
*Tar Heel player from 1969 through '71,
on Dean Smith*

When I was in Vietnam, he regularly wrote me and checked on my parents. I teasingly say that Michael Jordan and I are the two bookends on the Carolina basketball program. That's how little I played. Yet Coach Smith still treated me like a superstar.

Richard Vinroot

Tar Heel player (1962), mayor of Charlotte (1991–95)

☀ ☀ ☀

He tries to mask it and keep it inside, but he's a competitive sucker.

Larry Brown

guard (1961–63)/longtime college and NBA coach, on Dean Smith

☀ ☀ ☀

Coach Smith says the only time to be selfish is on offensive and defensive rebounds.

J. R. Reid

forward/center (1987–89)

D ean always made sure the players came first, before the athletic director, the chancellor, anyone! There were times I would call him and he would politely say, "John, I'm with a player right now, so we'll need to talk later." I always understood. It sent a tremendous message to his players.

John Swofford
*ACC commissioner/former UNC
athletic director*

P ractice is a privilege. If you're not here to work, don't come. This isn't a required freshman English course. This is fun and it's an elective. Not only that, it's easier than football.

Dean Smith

H e can throw chairs with his eyes.

Mitch Kupchak
on Smith

H e simply doesn't believe in luck. You win by being prepared, not by being lucky.

John Lotz
assistant coach (1966–72),
on Smith

T his was the only time I ever felt my job was to win. In fact, that's what I was told.

Dean Smith
on coaching the 1976 Olympic team

I haven't won a game at all. I've just happened to be the coach of some good teams.

Dean Smith

in 1983, on winning at least twenty games for the thirteenth straight year (1971–1983), an NCAA record that Smith would extend through 27 straight campaigns

When I met those guys, I saw how much respect they had for Coach Smith.

Clifford Rozier

forward (1991), after meeting former UNC stars Michael Jordan, James Worthy, and J. R. Reid. Rozier played at North Carolina for one season before transferring to Louisville

I can only speak for basketball, but we only recruit great people who are very good students. We'll take one exception a year to the general-admissions category, and that person has to be so highly recommended by his coach and his principal.

Dean Smith

In American society, you keep score, so they're going to keep a record. We never think in terms of who's going to get the points. We're worried about North Carolina getting the points.

Dean Smith

My first goal was to keep my job. Then I wanted to win. It was when I got more mature that I said, "What's most important is that we play well."

Dean Smith

I try to enter each season with a completely open mind. I never want to have my mind made up like I used to.

Dean Smith

on giving players playing time

◈ ◈ ◈

Interesting that we don't have time to play a two-out-of-three series or double elimination like baseball, but we would have a better chance of having the best team be champion.

Dean Smith

on the NCAA Tournament format

◈ ◈ ◈

Look, if someone offered you a job with *Sports Illustrated* and you were a junior in college, would you quit?

Dean Smith

to reporters, on why it makes sense for some players to depart early for the NBA

S ociety goes by the won-lost record too much. I think coaches get too much credit, and that's certainly true of me.

Dean Smith

❀ ❀ ❀

A thletic competition as we know it produces what is called the winner and the loser in our society. Those terms certainly have different connotations that aren't good. The loser and those associated with losing sometimes feel bad, and the winners have external affirmation for the wrong reasons. There can be values learned through competition. But a total emphasis on winning versus participation is the problem.

Dean Smith

❀ ❀ ❀

M y goal every year is to have the best team possible, and that's never changed. I never had any other goals than that.

Dean Smith

A ll I was after was our twenty-sixth, and we got it.

Dean Smith

On his eight hundredth career victory,
an 86–84 overtime win over Wake Forest
in the 1994 ACC Tourney semifinals

⚾ ⚾ ⚾

A ny game you lose in January and February isn't as important as the ones you lose in March [the NCAA Tournament]. You don't want to lose in March.

Dean Smith

⚾ ⚾ ⚾

S ome people don't think finishing first in the regular season means a lot anymore, but it is important. The tournament is three games and the regular season is fourteen. That's a lot tougher to win.

Dean Smith

I knew the words 'Dean Smith' before I could ever put a face to them.

Jerry Stackhouse
forward (1994–95),
who grew up as a Tar Heels fan

＊ ＊ ＊

Come-from-behind wins were so common under Smith that the Carolina media guide has a six-page section called "Fantastic Finishes."

Art Chansky

＊ ＊ ＊

I think you cannot do your job and say, "Here's the ball, gang," and the players will go out and they won't live up to their potential. A coach is supposed to bring them together as a team. What we do is discipline them first and then say, "Now you're free."

Dean Smith

SMITHOMETER READING:
INNOVATIONS FROM
THE MASTER

Because it was so critical to get into the correct defense after a made UNC basket before the opponent's next possession, Dean Smith came up with the "foul-line huddle"—an innovation that allowed his Tar Heels to assemble around the free throw shooter before a free throw or between free throws to get the all-important defensive signal from the bench.

Calling a timeout after a made basket to set up the right defense was another Smith original, especially late in the game. Eventually a rule change was instituted, stopping the clock after each field goal in the final minute of play, since precious time was often lost inbounding the ball by an opponent holding a lead.

Another Smith improvement was crediting the assist. Long dismayed by the attention a shooter received for making a basket when the man making the dish went unrecognized, Smith called for each Tar Heel scorer to point to the man who had fed him the ball as a sign of acknowledgment for the playmaker's unselfish play.

Players hesitate to take themselves out of games because they are afraid they won't get back in. Coach Smith's tired signal policy removed that fear because he allowed players to put themselves back in once they were rested. It encouraged fatigued players to come out of the game for the good of the team, an unselfish act.

Phil Ford

* * *

Smith's 1997 team was his last at Carolina. It started with three straight ACC losses and then rallied to win sixteen games in a row, the ACC championship, and an NCAA Final Four berth. Included was a win over Colorado in the NCAA tournament that gave Smith 877 victories, breaking the national record held by Adolph Rupp of Kentucky.

John Kilgo

* * *

Of all Dean Smith's statistics, perhaps his most impressive is his over 70 percent success rate in ACC road games.

Adam Lucas

L ong before Dean Smith brought Charlie Scott to North Carolina in 1966, his father was doing the same for black players in Emporia, Kansas. In 1934, Smith's dad had integrated the basketball team at Emporia High School.

Ken Rappoport

H e teaches more than basketball, he teaches you about life, about just being a part of society. He can do no wrong. Not in my book. Because he's done so much right for me. And, he's always very caring about the player as a person; not a basketball player, a person.

Michael Jordan
on Dean Smith

I wouldn't be where I am today without Coach Smith. I learned defense, how to block out, everything under him. I learned all the little things you need to be successful on and off the basketball court. He's a second father to many; not just myself, to many.

Michael Jordan

He gives you room to grow and to have responsibility. He really didn't want to spoon feed you, because he wasn't there to babysit, but at the same time he gave us direction and sat down with us all the time. Basketball wasn't the only thing he wanted us to do well.

Sam Perkins
on Dean Smith

H e brought out the best in you, because you knew coaching against a Dean Smith team would mean playing at a very high level, a championship level.

Mike Krzyzewski
Duke coach

H is age and gentlemanly manner had served him well with a team that was more mature, such as the 1997–98 Jamison and Carter group, but was not effective with a younger, less talented group, such as in 1998–99.

David DeWitt
on head coach Bill Guthridge

A s his assistant, I could make just about every decision I wanted to. And if I didn't want to make one, I could say, "Better go see Dean." So this year, if you see me get out my little portable phone with two minutes to go in a game, you'll know who I'm calling.

Bill Guthridge
on taking over the reins of the Tar Heel basketball program in the fall of 1997, after serving Dean Smith as an assistant for 30 years

I still think Coach Smith would be coaching if he didn't need to do all that other stuff. And I probably would be, too.

Bill Guthridge
on the peripheral duties of coaching: speaking engagements, conference meetings, conducting clinics, spring workouts, spring recruiting —all of which ultimately drained the two Tar Heel coaches

R oy Williams had been the slam-dunk [choice]. NBA wanderer Larry Brown, the most logical next option, had strong support from key members of the Tar Heel basketball family, but he was miffed that he had not been the first choice to replace Bill Guthridge; after his jump to the NBA in 1988, Kansas was placed on probation for violations during Brown's tenure, an unappealing detail to UNC. There was, it seemed, one potential compromise candidate who could solve most of Carolina's problems. And so, when [UNC Athletic Director] Baddour concluded his press conference after Williams's "I'm stayin'" announcement, he made just one phone call: Matt Doherty.

Adam Lucas

I n less than a month, Matt Doherty had brought in four new assistant coaches and dramatically altered the physical appearance of the basketball office. The message seemed clear: This isn't Dean Smith's program anymore.

Adam Lucas

M att Doherty came to North Carolina with a well-deserved reputation as a tough coach, even though he had only been the head man for one season at Notre Dame. . . . One day Doherty was so frustrated with his Fighting Irish team that he made the players run 304 consecutive sprints at practice. As a reminder of that brutal practice, some of the players wrote the number 304 on their sneakers. Not that they would ever forget.

Ken Rappoport

The freshmen—Jawad Williams, Melvin Scott, and Jackie Manuel—the hope for the future, were stunned to find that the suave, smiling coach who had recruited them often blistered them on the practice court. This confusion about Doherty's true personality caused an erosion of trust between players and coaching staff, which, combined with growing complaints about Doherty's management style, proved fatal.

Adam Lucas

The lack of trust crushed Doherty as his tenure wound down, because his players never felt comfortable telling him the truth about their concerns, instead telling him whatever they thought he wanted to hear.

Adam Lucas

W hich coach hasn't gotten criticism? I don't know of one.

Dean Smith
comparing his early years to Matt Doherty's up-and-down tenure at UNC (2000–03)

N ew-jack players. Matt yelled at 'em, but everybody gets yelled at. I wanted to quit my freshman year, too, but that's what happens. You don't go after the coach.

Michael Jordan

D ean Smith was more sarcastic when he wanted to get you to do something. Coach Guthridge was more laid-back. Coach Doherty is more fiery and vocal when he wants you to do something and get his point across.

Brendan Haywood
*center (1998–01),
on the three UNC coaches he played under*

T he first time I thought, "Wow, this guy is special," was with his work with the JV team. We'd have the junior varsity come and play defense against us, and each time they were so well taught.

Dean Smith

on his young junior assistant Roy Williams,
in the late 1970s

H e's somebody you cheer for. He's been here a lot and I've always wanted him to win. But we didn't want him to win tonight.

Bruce Weber

on Roy Williams, after UNC had just downed
Illinois in the 2005 NCAA championship game

I 'm pretty darn corny. I can cry at the drop of a hat.

Roy Williams

R oy, you're going to be crying tonight.

Anonymous fan
*to Roy Williams before the 2005
NCAA championship game against Illinois*

FAST BREAK: *Williams is notorious for his unabashed emotionalism, particularly during press conferences.*

W hen I've been so emotional after
losses, it's because I've felt I had let
those kids down.

Roy Williams

W ork the ball inside often enough,
he is fond of saying, and you will
eventually get the other team in foul trouble, which enables you to play against sub-
stitutes rather than starters in the game's
crucial minutes.

Adam Lucas
*on a basic tenet of Roy Williams's coaching
philosophy*

We have one very simple rule here. Do what I tell you to do. I don't give a crap why you did it wrong. It's a very simple rule: do what I tell you to do.

Roy Williams

* * *

Roy Williams's ability to critique a player while maintaining his respect is key, as is his résumé, which included 418 victories at Kansas.

Adam Lucas

* * *

Respect everyone and fear no one.

Roy Williams

* * *

I knew there were some times when they walked out of practice united in their anger against me. I was fine with that.

Roy Williams
*on cultivating team unity with his wildly
erratic, extremely talented Tar Heel team of
2003–04, inherited from the Doherty regime*

S mith and Williams are bound more tightly than Smith and Wesson.

Grant Wahl

on the enduring, close relationship between Dean Smith and Roy Williams

※ ※ ※

H e's much more innovative. I copy people.

Roy Williams

comparing his coaching style with that of longtime mentor Dean Smith

※ ※ ※

I 'm the kind of coach who likes five passes and a dead layup.

Roy Williams

It's a beautiful game. . . . I think we've been demanding teachers, and caring, I hope. All of the coaching staff. The guys don't believe it some nights, but we really do care. I think I learn every year. I learn about young people and human nature. Until I get senile, I think I'm a better coach every year.

Dean Smith

SHRINE TO
NO. 23

T his person walks up to me and says, "Do you know Michael Jordan?" I said, "Yes." He said, "Could you write down on a piece of paper that you know him?"

Chris Brust

Tar Heel player from 1979 through '82,
on an incident that occurred stemming from
Brust's association as a member of the '82
national champion Carolina team

T here is a once-in-a-lifetime thing going on here. He has to be a combination of Babe Ruth, Santa Claus, and Elvis.

Bob Greene
*columnist, Chicago Tribune,
on Jordan's popularity*

❋ ❋ ❋

O n February 17, 1963, God wanted to do something special, so he created Michael.

James Jordan
father of Michael Jordan

❋ ❋ ❋

H e was God disguised as Michael Jordan.

Larry Bird
Boston Celtic legend

❋ ❋ ❋

T he best ever. Period.

Newsweek

It was embarrassing, not making that team. They posted the roster, and it was there a long, long time without my name on it. I remember being really mad. Whenever I was working out and got tired and figured I ought to stop, I'd close my eyes and see that list in the locker room without my name on it, and that usually got me going again.

Michael Jordan

on being cut from his high school team before his sophomore year at Laney High in Wilmington, North Carolina, in 1978

I wanted to learn how to cook and clean and sew and all that. I figured no girl would ever want to marry me, and I didn't know if I'd have enough money to eat out.

Michael Jordan

on why he took home economics
in high school

That's the best six-four player I've ever seen!

Roy Williams

then-assistant coach to Dean Smith,
on seeing Michael Jordan for the first time at
a UNC basketball camp for high schoolers
in 1980

Bill Guthridge [assistant coach] had seen Michael play in February of his junior year in high school and thought he might be an ACC player, because he was such a good athlete—six-foot-three, quick, though at that time he played inside not outside. Then Michael came to our basketball camp that summer, and [assistants] Roy Williams and Eddie Fogler mentioned him to me: "Gosh, that Wilmington kid is really quick, and he's so dedicated."

Dean Smith

The kid who had grown up a David Thompson fan rooting against Carolina had decided to become a Tar Heel.

Art Chansky

*on Jordan's decision to sign with
North Carolina*

I told him, "This young man is well put together. He really sees the big picture." Then I remember telling Dean Smith, "I just hope he can play basketball."

Bruce Ogilvie

sports psychologist,
on evaluating freshman Michael Jordan
in 1981

❈ ❈ ❈

I thought I would go in and be a flop. Everyone was expecting so much. [But Dean Smith] said to treat it like something you really enjoy and not to treat it like a job.

Michael Jordan

❈ ❈ ❈

Michael Jordan isn't Al Wood, but he's a great freshman prospect.

Dean Smith

in reference to the just-graduated senior
All-America guard/forward Wood

When we would scrimmage, we always put Michael on the team with the bench guys. We did it to make sure he remembered he was a freshman. You could tell right away that he had game, but what made him special was that he just hated to lose.

Sam Perkins

You haven't proven anything yet like the others.

Dean Smith

to the freshman Jordan, whom Smith refused to let be photographed with his four upper-classmen starters for the cover of Sports Illustrated, which had picked the Tar Heels No. 1 in preseason of 1981–82

When I saw my name up on the board to start, I couldn't believe it. I was nervous. But I went out and made the first shot, and started to settle down.

Michael Jordan

on starting for North Carolina in his very first game as a freshman in the fall of 1981. Jordan, ironically, wound up making the first shot of the season as well as the last for the eventual national champion Tar Heels

When I came to the University of North Carolina, you saw two people in me, my mother and my father. Now you don't just see my mother and father; you also see Dean Smith.

Michael Jordan

JORDAN AND THE
NAME GAME

Michael Jordan wasn't always, well, Michael Jordan. During his high school days in Wilmington, North Carolina, as well as his freshman year at North Carolina, Jordan went more familiarly by the name Mike. His Tar Heel teammates were split, with some calling him Mike and others calling him Michael.

Noticing the disparity and needing clarification for the team's 1981–82 media guide, former UNC Sports Information Director Rick Brewer decided to go directly to the source and see which appellation Jordan himself preferred.

Jordan was of little help: "I don't care; it doesn't make any difference to me. Call me whatever you want."

Brewer replied that he felt Michael Jordan had more of a ring to it than just plain Mike. Jordan said fine, and the rest, as we know now, is history.

H e was very gregarious, very confident. As a freshman, Michael was a very serious kid. Very neat. His clothes looked nice. They were always neatly pressed. He was very aware of his presence. He always had a clean haircut and things like that. He really listened—he was a good listener. And he played hard.

Matt Doherty

Jordan's teammate on the 1982 national championship team

S mith considered Jordan his best offensive rebounder and the number-one option when a zone defense denied Worthy and Perkins the ball. Without him, the Tar Heels would never have survived the ACC Tournament in Greensboro.

Art Chansky

on Jordan as a freshman in 1981–82

I remember after practice we were playing chicken, where each guy would take the ball at the hash mark and dribble in, and the other would try to block it, and you would try to dunk. I remember him dunking on me, but I remember dunking on him. That changed quickly. I didn't want to play chicken after his freshman year. He really grew up, physically and mentally. His game really expanded between his freshman and sophomore years. He became a man.

Matt Doherty
on Michael Jordan

My jumping ability has a lot of creativity, and it adds to the admiration of most fans, because fans like the dunk; they like creative things.

Michael Jordan

ometimes, with creativity, you don't know what's going to happen. Not in my game, anyway.

Michael Jordan

he spins, the reverses, the fall-aways, the double-pumps, the leaping leaners, the glides. Then there were the dunks: the cradle jam, the rock-a-baby, the tomahawk, and the leaner. That was the one where Jordan turned his body sideways and seemed to look down in the basket. He executed them all with his tongue hanging out, a habit he picked up from his father.

Donald W. Patterson

writer

W e told him Coach Smith wouldn't like him running around with his tongue hanging out. I told him, "You're going to bite on it one day." And, sure enough, one day he did. We all said, "We told you so."

Sam Perkins

to Jordan, who even in college exhibited his famous tongue wag

M y, oh my, did he ever pick things up fast! That's one of the many special things about Michael.

Dean Smith

I did hold [Michael Jordan] back. I said, "Throw the ball inside. Sam Perkins is shooting 59 percent; Michael's shooting 54 percent."

Dean Smith

B ack then, Michael wasn't the jump-shooter he is now. But he could elevate and hang over everybody to get a dunk or a layup. Why shoot a jumper when you can do that?

Sam Perkins

commenting on teammate Jordan's days at North Carolina during the height of Jordan's NBA career

W hen I came back down to the floor, I said to myself, "Was that really me?"

Michael Jordan

on a confidence-boosting monster dunk over seven-foot Geff Crompton and former All-America forward Al Wood, in a pickup game before the start of practice Jordan's freshman year at Carolina

E ver since I made that shot, everything has just fallen into place for me. Everything has been perfect. It was destiny. If that shot hadn't gone in, I don't think I would be where I am today.

Michael Jordan

on "The Shot": his 1982 championship-game-winning left-side jumper as a freshman, with 15 seconds remaining, that beat Georgetown

❋ ❋ ❋

W hen he got the ball, I was open at the free-throw line, and I joked that if he had passed me the ball, I would have knocked down the shot and everybody would have been talking about Doherty, not Air Jordan. Of course, we know that's not true.

Matt Doherty

on teammate Michael Jordan's celebrated game-winning shot in the 1982 NCAA championship game

I t's hard to put into focus. What I remember is a skinny freshman that most teams left alone as a freshman.

Dean Smith
*on Jordan, who started as a freshman
for Smith in 1982*

I want to see if anybody in the world can be better than Mike. Mike said it himself: Somebody will be greater than him. I'm not saying it's me, but I wish it was. It's all about being competitive and trying to have that spirit, to be the best you can be.

Rashad McCants
on his idol Jordan

Michael Jordan, the least hyped two-time player of the year in college basketball history.

Ken Rappoport

In my rookie [NBA] season, it got to the point where I missed college and all the things that you learn through that system, all the unity that went on with being a part of that team. So I said, "Hey, I'll put these shorts on," and it gives me a good sense of home, a good remembrance. . . . I don't go anywhere without them. That means I'm carrying a piece of North Carolina wherever I go. It really makes me feel at home. I wear them everywhere I go—under suits, pants, shorts, my uniform—everywhere.

Michael Jordan

FAST BREAK: UNC sees to it that Jordan receives plenty of blue-and-white shorts.

I tell you the one thing that separated him. He improved his speed and his jumping ability. He grew two inches between his freshman and sophomore years. Every drill we did, he would listen and go do it. When our drills start out, they're not competitive. Once we have them, they become competitive. Then he had to win the drill. When you put that athleticism with that determination and then that huge competitive heart and savvy, you know he's going to be good. His big jump, though, was between his freshman and sophomore years. He was winning everything his sophomore year.

Dean Smith
on Michael Jordan

JORDAN CHOOSES
TAR HEELS EXPERIENCE
OVER NBA BULLS

In a 2005 article published in Cigar Aficionado, *basketball icon Michael Jordan,
interviewed by Marvin R. Shanken, the magazine's editor/publisher, was asked which
brought him more pleasure, playing for
North Carolina or the Chicago Bulls.*

*"I would say it was the Tar Heels," M. J.
stated. "No one knew me until then. That's
when the notoriety and everything began
with Michael Jordan.*

*"Up to that point, everybody had heard
that this kid is pretty good, but we don't
know how good. . . . The University of
North Carolina really gave me the foundation that it took to become a basketball
player. Up to then, I hadn't been spoiled by
the media spotlight. I was still raw.*

*"As a result, I had an appetite to prove to
everybody that I was a decent basketball
player, or a good enough basketball player
to be at North Carolina."*

Jordan was then asked if he ever regretted leaving Carolina after his junior season.

"Yeah, because I had a great time in college," he said. "It was the first time I'd been away from home. I'd met new people and made new friends. It was an exciting time. It was just fun."

Jordan then spoke of Dean Smith's role in his decision to jump to the pros early.

"It was Coach Dean Smith's call. I relied so much on his knowledge," Jordan said. "The NBA was an area where I wasn't too knowledgeable. . . . It was a great opportunity. Coach Smith felt that it would be the best opportunity for me to make it in professional basketball. Once he researched the situation, to find out where I would go in the draft, then I started weighing the pros and cons.

"You get the chance to mature in college. . . . College teaches you a lot. It teaches you about being on your own, making decisions, and even handling bank accounts. Eventually, you're going to have to deal with those things anyway."

If you were going to invent the prototype for the athlete for the nineties, you would create an athlete who is articulate, clean-cut but not too square, with just enough spice to be fun, who is in touch with the community, who cuts across demographic boundaries, who has diverse skills, who is genuine and overall is fun to watch play. When you got finished, you'd have Michael.

David Falk
Jordan's agent

I worked hard.

Michael Jordan

MAJOR
MOMENTS

I t was a classic game, one that would earn distinction as one of the greatest NCAA final games ever played. Moments from that game are burned not only in the minds of Tar Heel fans but in the memories of all sport aficionados: Patrick Ewing goaltending Carolina's first five shots . . . Worthy's incredible scoring duel with fellow Gastonia native Sleepy Floyd . . . Jordan hitting The Shot . . . Fred Brown's ill-advised pass.

David DeWitt

on the Tar Heels' win over Georgetown
in the 1982 national championship game

I t was one of the greatest man-to-man defensive exhibitions I've ever seen.

Frank McGuire

on guard Bobby Cunningham's (1956–58) performance against South Carolina's Grady Wallace, the nation's leading scorer in 1957. Cunningham personally held Wallace to just one field goal

I told the guys we got a bad break, but we had come too far to quit now. We had to want it more.

Frank McGuire

on star forward Lennie Rosenbluth fouling out late in the second half of the 1957 NCAA championship game against Kansas and Wilt Chamberlain, an affair that would go into triple overtime, before the Tar Heels ultimately prevailed 54–53

M any basketball historians consider the 1957 North Carolina-Kansas show-down to be the greatest NCAA championship game ever played.

John Nichols

※ ※ ※

I got it and I knew the ceiling was way up there. I knew there were four or five seconds left, and I knew that if I could get it up high enough, when it came down the game would be over.

Tommy Kearns
guard (1956–58),
on running out the final seconds of the 1957
NCAA championship game in Kansas City
Municipal Auditorium. UNC defeated Kansas and
sensational Jayhawk center Wilt Chamberlain
in triple overtime, 54–53. With six seconds left,
Carolina deflected an inbounds pass by Kansas,
setting up Kearns's stratospheric heave

O ne of the greatest [moments] was the monumental upset of unbeaten and top-ranked South Carolina on January 4, 1971, when the Tar Heels held the ball and forced Frank McGuire's Gamecocks out of the zone, ran them ragged, and posted the stunning 79–64 win. That game ushered in a new era of invincibility for Smith's program—and paved the way for a number of other "unforgettables."

Art Chansky

W here were you when Walter Davis's twenty-eight-foot shot sent a game against Duke into overtime in 1974, after the Tar Heels had trailed by eight points with seventeen seconds left? The Tar Heels went on to win.

David Scott
author

T he quintessential Carmichael Auditorium game took place on March 2, 1974, the annual renewal of the rivalry with Duke University. On that day, the Blue Devils built an 86–78 lead with just 17 seconds remaining. These were the days before the three-point shot, so an eight-point deficit required four possessions, an almost impossible feat in less than 20 seconds. But the Heels tied the game on a Walter Davis 30-footer at the end of regulation and eventually captured a 96–92 overtime victory.

Adam Lucas

Wouldn't it be fun to come back and win this game? Here's how we're going to do it.

Dean Smith

to his Tar Heel players just before the close of the historic March 2, 1974, comeback against Duke, in which North Carolina, down by eight points with only seventeen seconds left, executed two Bobby Jones free throws, converted a steal, and forced another turnover ending with Walter Davis's two-pointer. After a missed Duke free throw, Davis's 34-foot buzzer-beater pushed the game into overtime. UNC went on to post a miraculous 96–92 win, the largest comeback in the shortest amount of time ever recorded in the history of college basketball

E ven the scoreboard was playing defense for the Tar Heels.

Anonymous observer

after Carolina's phenomenal come-from-behind overtime 101–100 victory over Wake Forest in the 1975 ACC Tournament. Trailing the Demon Deacons by eight points with 50 seconds remaining, the Heels converted three Wake Forest turnovers, including an errant Wake pass that skimmed the overhead scoreboard in Greensboro Coliseum. Brad Hoffman's jumper with one second left knotted it, and UNC went on to grab the big win in OT

THE ULTIMATE STALL:
UNC GOES SCORELESS
FOR A HALF AGAINST DUKE

Leave it to the inventors of the famous Four Corners offense to take the delay tactic to the ultimate extreme.

In the days before the shot clock, in a battle against archrival Duke, on February 24, 1979, UNC went scoreless in the first half, while employing a classic stall. Score at the end of the first 20 minutes: Duke 7, North Carolina 0!

Of course, the Tar Heels' plan had been to try and force the Blue Devils to leave their zone, to come out and go after them, thus hopefully creating backdoor opportunities under the basket. That never materialized, so coach Dean Smith was forced to open up the Carolina offense in the second half, in what turned out to be a dead-even standoff, with both teams tallying 40 points.

Duke, with its seven-point first-half margin gained at the hands of UNC's Four Corners delay, won the game, 47–40.

B ehind Al Wood's astonishing 39 points, the Tar Heels had rudely ousted Virginia and Ralph Sampson from the Final Four. It had been a bitter defeat for the Cavaliers, who had twice rallied to beat the Heels during the regular season.

Art Chansky

on North Carolina's 1981 team that advanced to the NCAA finals, only to lose to Indiana

W ith Virginia packing under the basket in the nationally televised final, Jordan nailed four jumpers that kept Carolina alive in a game that seemed to be slipping away. . . . Worthy and Perkins could not get free inside the zone, so Smith called on his freshman to take the biggest shots of his basketball career.

Art Chansky

on the 1982 ACC Tournament finals

THE VIRGINIA BATTLES
IN THE RALPH SAMPSON ERA

*Three of the greatest games in Carolina his-
tory featured big wins over the University of
Virginia and Ralph Sampson, two of them
comebacks, during the 1982 and '83 seasons. Sampson, a dominating 7–1 two-time
Player of the Year, had transformed the Cavaliers into a legitimate national champion
candidate.*

*The Tar Heels, down by 16 points, rallied to
defeat Virginia at Chapel Hill, 65–60, on January 9, 1982, but lost by 16 at Charlottesville
a month later. The teams would meet in a
rubber match at the ACC Tournament finals,
in which North Carolina elected to go into its
famous Four Corners delay with 7:34 remaining and barely leading, at 44–43. The tactic
worked to perfection, though, with UNC posting a 47–45 victory on Matt Doherty's three
free throws in the last 28 seconds.*

*The following year, Sampson and Company
had built a strong 16-point lead at Carmichael Auditorium, before Michael Jordan
resurrected the Tar Heels in the final minute
with a follow shot, a steal, a dunk, and a
rebound over Sampson, as Carolina took a
64–63 win.*

W e almost took James Madison for granted. . . . They deserved to win, because they had us.

James Worthy

on the near-upset of top-seeded North Carolina in the second round of the 1982 NCAA East Regionals. Worthy scored the Tar Heels' final five points, and UNC held on for a 52–50 victory

✦ ✦ ✦

C arolina came close to not reaching the championship game against Georgetown. After holding a double-digit lead on Houston in Saturday's semifinal, the Heels had to stave off a Cougar rally sparked by Clyde Drexler. Finally, Worthy's driving dunk late in the second half cemented a return to the Monday night title game.

Art Chansky

on the 1982 Final Four semifinals

K nock it in, Michael!

Dean Smith,
*to Michael Jordan, before the freshman's
NCAA championship-winning jump shot in
1982 against Georgetown*

* * *

O f all that has been written and recited about that epic against John Thompson's Hoyas—Worthy's determination and dominating performance, Jordan's winning shot—the key was Smith's ability to lift the pressure of finally "winning the big one" for him from his players' shoulders.

Art Chansky
on the 1982 NCAA champions

* * *

H e was as loose before and during the game as I ever remembered him. To the rest of us, if we had lost, suicide would have been an option.

Eddie Fogler
*assistant coach (1972–86),
on his boss, Dean Smith, before and during
the 1982 NCAA championship game
against Georgetown*

J ordan later admitted closing his eyes as the biggest basket of Dean Smith's career left his hands, perhaps symbolizing the blind confidence his coach had put in him before the season and the dream he had the night before of taking the winning shot.

Art Chansky

on the game-winner against Georgetown in the 1982 NCAA finals

J ames Worthy played his greatest college game, hitting thirteen of seventeen shots against Georgetown, including four consecutive monster dunks in the second half.

Art Chansky

on the UNC All-American's performance in the 1982 NCAA championship game

I was ecstatic because we won, but I don't think it meant I was any better a coach.

Dean Smith

following the Heels' 1982 national title game win over Georgetown

W e were lucky to be there, to get by Houston. My thinking is that you had to be very lucky and very good. It isn't the best four out of seven. Who knows whether we would have won it if it had been four out of seven? But that's the magic of the NCAA Tournament. You don't necessarily get the best team to win the championship. On several occasions the best team hasn't. Fortunately, I think we played extremely well in that game. And Georgetown played extremely well. It has to be one of the finest games, two teams really playing at the top of their games.

Dean Smith

on the 1982 NCAA championship game duel against Georgetown

O ne legend—Smith's—was cemented, while another one was born.

David DeWitt

on the close of the 1982 NCAA finals—
North Carolina's championship game win over
Georgetown—in which UNC freshman
Michael Jordan bucketed a clutch last-minute
jumper to give Dean Smith his first
NCAA crown

I felt like I was a part of that, too. It's a whole family, everybody can enjoy that and share in it.

Walter Davis

forward (1974–77),
on sharing the moment with the 1982 team's
national crown triumph

O kay, we've got them right where we want them.

Dean Smith

huddling with his No. 1-ranked Tar Heels, on January 19, 1986, trailing Marquette in Milwaukee by seven points, with under four minutes to play. UNC played tight defense, forcing the Warriors into a pair of turnovers, and repeatedly fouled Marquette, who failed to convert the free throws. North Carolina came away with a 66–64 victory

C arolina and Duke played one of the most heated ACC Tournament finals in history in 1989, but it was almost overshadowed by the off-court battle between the two coaches. After taking offense at "J. R. Can't Reid" signs at Cameron that he felt were racially motivated, Dean Smith pointed out that the combined SAT scores of Reid and fellow Tar Heel Scott Williams were higher than those of Duke's Christian Laettner and Danny Ferry.

Adam Lucas

FAST BREAK: The feud between Duke's Krzyzewski and UNC's Smith was launched by a comment the Duke coach made that two sets of rules were in existence in the ACC: one for UNC and one for everybody else. Smith, livid at the signs in Cameron attacking Carolina center J. R. Reid, countered with the above-mentioned SAT comparisons between his Tar Heel phenoms and the two Blue Devil stars, both of whom were recruited by Smith, hence the knowledge of their SAT scores.

T he Tar Heels play the underdog role to perfection against top-seeded OU, capped by Fox's late banker.

Dick Vitale

ESPN the Magazine,
on Rick Fox's coolness under pressure against
Oklahoma in the 1990 NCAA Midwest
Regionals, won by North Carolina, 79–77.
Vitale rated the moment No. 7 on his all-time
NCAA Tournament "Shockers" list

H aving a nickname and a lot of press clippings doesn't score any points on the basketball court. If they want it, they are going to have to earn it.

George Lynch

forward (1990–93),
on Michigan's "Fab Five," heavily favored to
take the 1993 NCAA championship game.
The Tar Heels shocked the Wolverines, 77–71,
for Dean Smith's second national title

M uch has been made since Chris Webber's infamous timeout [and resulting technical foul] with Michigan trailing by two and eleven seconds left to play. But Dean Smith knew it was hardly an unforced error, as great defense by Derrick Phelps and George Lynch had forced Webber into panic and to call a timeout his team didn't have. It was no different from harassing him into a travel or bad shot.

Art Chansky

I t took a couple instances of good fortune for North Carolina basketball, under Smith, to attain the game's ultimate goal: a national championship. In 1982, it was an errant pass by Georgetown's Fred Brown; in 1993, it was a timeout called by Michigan's Chris Webber—when the Wolverines had no more timeouts remaining. Both gaffes came at the ends of national championship games and obscured, in some minds, the heights achieved by those and other Carolina teams. In the television age, people remember moments, not extended periods of excellence.

David DeWitt

T here ain't much more to be said but we're number one.

Donald Williams

shooting guard (1992–95),
who hit five of seven three-pointers,
including North Carolina's final four points on
free throws, in scoring 25 points during the
77–71 win over Michigan in the 1993 NCAA
finals. Williams, who also bucketed 25 points
and again hit on five of seven three-pointers
in the Final Four semifinal win over Kansas,
was named the tournament's
Most Outstanding Player

I f you didn't like that, you don't like college basketball.

Dean Smith

*on the Tar Heels' 102–100 double overtime
victory over Duke in 1995*

❀ ❀ ❀

G et the ball inside. Let the Big Dog eat.

Roy Williams

*on UNC strategy to get the ball to
center/forward Sean May in the 2005 NCAA
championship game against Illinois*

❀ ❀ ❀

T hat steal was the key to the game. After that we could see the doubt in their eyes.

Sean May

*on Raymond Felton's critical steal of Illinois
forward Luther Head's errant pass to salt away
the 2005 NCAA championship game, 75–70.
The Tar Heels held the Illini scoreless over the
last two and a half minutes*

NORTH CAROLINA
TAR HEELS
ALL-TIME TEAM

S *electing the North Carolina men's basketball all-time team is surely an exercise in exasperation, if not madness. It is truly a humbling experience. James Worthy, Billy Cunningham, Kenny Smith, Charlie Scott, Vince Carter, Bob McAdoo, Brad Daugherty, Larry Miller, Walter Davis, Jerry Stackhouse . . . and that's just part of the long list of Tar Heel greats who didn't make the final cut!*

Four members of our all-time five can be found among the current list of UNC record-holders, including one prolific forward who still owns a passel of marks from his days in Chapel Hill almost 50 years ago. Interestingly, the one player on the hallowed unit not in the company of these standard-bearers is the iconic Michael Jordan. But it's unlikely you'll hear too many of the Carolina faithful quibbling over that detail.

LENNIE ROSENBLUTH

forward (1954–57; Captain '57)

National Player of the Year (Helms Foundation, 1957);
consensus All-America (1957);
All-ACC (1955, '56, '57);
still holds UNC records for both season (28.0)
and career (26.9) scoring average;
one of only three players ever to be named
ACC Player of the Year, ACC Tournament MVP,
NCAA Regional MVP, and National Player of the Year
in the same season

H is ability to hit clutch shots set him apart from others. Also had an uncanny ability to hit the off-balance shot. Was adept at drawing fouls from the opposition. His most famous play was probably against Wake Forest in the ACC Tournament final as a senior [in 1957], when he hit a hook shot, was fouled, and completed the three-point play to give UNC the win and a bid to the NCAA Tournament.

Carolina: 2004–05 Tar Heels
Basketball

Lennie Rosenbluth

ANTAWN JAMISON
forward (1996–98)

Unanimous National Player of the Year (1998);
Naismith Award winner (1998);
John Wooden Award winner (1998);
consensus All-America (1998);
ACC Player of the Year (1998);
ACC Tournament MVP (1998)

A ntawn Jamison really has quickness, great work habits and exceptional hands, and he moves his feet well. At the next level of play he may be a small forward, taking people off the dribble. . . . He has a huge heart, which is always important.

Dean Smith

I t's every kid's dream to go to the NB— . . . Final Four.

Antawn Jamison

his inadvertent slip of the tongue at a press conference before North Carolina's participation in the 1997 NCAA Final Four. Jamison had been hounded by reports of a possible jump to the NBA after his sophomore season. The Tar Heel star stayed another year, capturing National Player of the Year honors and leading the Heels to a second consecutive NCAA Final Four appearance

Antawn Jamison

SAM PERKINS

center (1981–84)

Three-time All-America (1982–84);
National Player of the Year finalist (1984),;
three-time All-ACC (1982–84);
ACC Rookie of the Year (1981)

F rom the first few pick-up games, it was pretty obvious that Sam was a special player.

Matt Doherty

on Sam Perkins

◉ ◉ ◉

H e's probably, looking back, the first time we've had a true shotblocker. That gives you a dimension that just does wonders.

Dean Smith

on Perkins,
second all-time in North Carolina shot-
blocking annals, with 245. Perkins is also the
Tar Heels' leading career rebounder (1,167)

Sam Perkins

PHIL FORD

point guard (1975–78)

Three-time All-America (1976–78);
UNC's all-time leading scorer (2,290 points);
ACC Player of the Year (1978);
two-time ACC Athlete of the Year (1977, '78);
member 1976 U.S. Olympic gold medal-winning
basketball team

I admit the Four Corners wasn't fair with Phil Ford. He hit his foul shots, he could drive, he could take it in, bring it out, and pass it off. He was unstoppable.

Dean Smith

Michael Jordan was a great player at Carolina from 1981 to 1984, but he was not the greatest player in school history. That title goes to Phil Ford, who scored more points and held a more secure place in the hearts of Carolina fans when he left UNC.

David DeWitt

Phil Ford

MICHAEL JORDAN

shooting guard (1982–84)

Two-time National Player of the Year (1983, '84);
All-America (1984);
two-time All-ACC (1983, '84)

The legendary Michael Jordan began his unparalleled basketball career by hitting the game-winning shot as a freshman in the Tar Heels' 1982 national championship game. With incredible body control and a vertical leap of close to four feet, he truly earned the nickname of "Air" Jordan. The young star was named the National Player of the Year his last two seasons.

John Nichols

❄ ❄ ❄

He told me he knew that he was going to take that last shot to win it. Knew it. Dreamed about it. Most of all, he wanted it. He wanted the ball in that situation. How many freshmen would have that confidence to take it, then make it?

Davis Love III

PGA Tour golfer and a fellow student with Jordan at North Carolina

Michael Jordan

DEAN SMITH

coach (1962–97)

Winningest basketball coach in
NCAA Division I history (879);
Basketball Hall of Fame (1983);
two national championships (1982, '93);
eight-time ACC Coach of the Year;
won at least 20 games for 27 straight years;
made a record 23 consecutive appearances
in the NCAA Tournament

I n his thirty-six years at Carolina, Smith's teams won or shared a record seventeen ACC championships, won thirteen ACC tournaments, won national championships in 1982 and 1993, and never was cited for an NCAA infraction. A full 97 percent of Smith's players at Carolina received degrees and nearly half of those went on to further study. In 1982, Smith was inducted into the Basketball Hall of Fame.

John Kilgo

※ ※ ※

H e's the best there is on the court, but he's even better off the court in what he gives to those who come into contact with him.

Roy Williams
on Smith

Dean Smith

NORTH CAROLINA
TAR HEELS
ALL-TIME TEAM

Lennie Rosenbluth, *forward*

Antawn Jamison, *forward*

Sam Perkins, *center*

Phil Ford, *point guard*

Michael Jordan, *shooting guard*

Dean Smith, *coach*

THE GREAT
TAR HEEL
FIVES

T he 2005 team was a *team.*

Roy Williams

T he "White Phantoms," one of the great early North Carolina teams, raced to the 1923–24 national championship with a 26–0 record. The up-tempo Phantoms, led by Jack "Sprat" Cobb, Cart Carmichael, Monk McDonald, and Bill Dodderer, were the early basketball version of Lakers Showtime. They had very few close games, usually outscoring opponents by a composite 2-to-1 margin.

Ken Rappoport

T hat 1924 team was characterized by quickness and speed. It was a very, very fast team, and we used the fast break effectively.

Norman Shepard

T here was no NCAA tournament [until 1939], so the national champion was determined by the vote of an organization called the Helms Foundation. Based on North Carolina's perfect season, the Helms Foundation declared the Tar Heels national champions in 1924.

John Nichols

❖ ❖ ❖

I n 1946, the Tar Heels won 30 games and went all he way to the NCAA finals before losing to Oklahoma A&M [43–40]. That team featured funnyman Horace "Bones" McKinney and John "Hook" Dillon, whose hook-shot artistry was the talk of Madison Square Garden. McKinney was the Tar Heels' court jester, and his quick wit kept his teammates laughing all the way to the NCAA finals.

Ken Rappoport

T he best ever? Somebody had better at least mention the 1957 Carolina team that went 32–0 and beat Kansas and Wilt Chamberlain in three overtimes for the national championship.

John Kilgo

I thought for sure we would lose at least four games we won and finally I almost hoped we would get beaten just to take the terrific pressure off the players. Well, not the players so much, because they kept cool even if I didn't. . . . Everyone was waiting for them to crack, but these kids wouldn't. The players seemed to take the pressure far better than the fans or I did.

Frank McGuire

on the rigors of the 1957 undefeated season

T he pressure was tremendous. It was similar to a pitcher nearing a no-hitter in baseball.

Frank McGuire

on the mental weariness of attempting to go through a season undefeated, which his national champion Tar Heels accomplished in 1957 (32–0)

* * *

T he McGuire era peaked with the unde-feated national championship season of 1956–57 in which Lennie Rosenbluth and his supporting cast won two consecutive triple-overtime games in the Final Four—overcoming Kansas and Wilt Chamberlain in the final—to capture the national championship.

David DeWitt

* * *

T he 1982 Tar Heels don't come in second to any team. They did everything they had to do. After losing that big game at Virginia [74–58, February 3], they closed with 16 straight wins.

John Kilgo

W e respected each other. On a team, you don't always have to be best friends with everybody; you don't always have to hang out with everybody. But I think we got along well. We had good leadership with Jimmy Black and James Worthy. We were all pretty serious about it—and unselfish. James could have averaged 30 points per game if he wanted to. But his personality was great. He's a very welcoming guy. James would make everybody feel comfortable. We just wanted to win. We didn't have that much depth, but we had great balance.

Matt Doherty

on the 1982 national champion Tar Heels

This championship [1982] is a memory that no one will ever be able to take away from us. Years from now when they talk about Carolina basketball, they will talk about this team as if it just played yesterday.

Matt Doherty

🌼 🌼 🌼

We were all thrown there for a reason. They sprinkled some magic dust over us, and they said this is what's going to happen that year. It was destiny.

Jimmy Black
on the 1982 national championship team

🌼 🌼 🌼

If we had won in 1981, I think it would have been very hard to win in '82. However, if we hadn't been in the Final Four in '81, we might have been just happy to be in the Final Four [in '82].

Dean Smith

THE BLUE TEAM

Onetime LSU football coach Paul Dietzel's 1958 national champions may have had their Chinese Bandits third-string defense, but around Chapel Hill, North Carolina, nobody out-hustles the Tar Heels' Blue Team.

Conceived one night in a game against Georgia Tech when the regular starters were flat, Coach Dean Smith inserted his hustling second-stringers, who pressed and hassled the Yellow Jackets, tiring them and setting them up for the well-rested, returning first-stringers.

"I just threw those guys in, and they really got it going," said Smith after that game. "They were stealing the ball and scoring. They almost caught up."

Thus was born the famous Blue Team, an aggregate of UNC bench warmers who, under the Smith school of Carolina basketball, exemplified in every way the word hustle.

A nd how about 1984? Had Kenny Smith, the freshman point guard starter, not broken his wrist against LSU in Chapel Hill, this could have been the best. This team killed good teams before the Smith injury. That injury to Smith occurred on January 29th, and Carolina was 17–0.

John Kilgo

W ith the Final Four scheduled for New Orleans, Dean Smith placed a doctored photo of the Superdome in each player's locker on the first day of practice. The overhead message board read "1993 NCAA Champions North Carolina."

Art Chansky

W e may not have been the most glamorous team, but we proved we were the best.

Donald Williams
*Final Four MVP in the 1993
NCAA Tournament,
on the '93 'Heels*

C all us lucky, but also call us national champions.

Dean Smith

on gaining his second NCAA crown, defeating Michigan, 77–71 in 1993, after Wolverines star Chris Webber's mental gaffe of calling a timeout with 11 seconds to play when Michigan had no more timeouts

⚜ ⚜ ⚜

D ean's ball clubs were like Swiss watches. Never a flutter, never a rattle—always smooth and brutally efficient.

Al McGuire

late former head coach of Marquette/ TV analyst

⚜ ⚜ ⚜

W e're ready to be not a good team, but a great team.

Sean May

on the 2004 Tar Heels, in their first season under new head coach Roy Williams

I ndividuals like Sean May and Raymond Felton provided the unit with its heart and soul, and freshman Marvin Williams was its constant surprise.

S. L. Price

senior writer, Sports Illustrated,
on the 2005 national champion Tar Heels

❀ ❀ ❀

R oy Williams's achievement with this team was more subtle than mere winning, and it shouldn't be underestimated. Williams walked the tightrope between Tar Heels traditionalism and a team that had overthrown it. He convinced the team's most prominent rebel—not to mention its offensive star—to shoot less and pass more, and if Rashad McCants didn't always dive for loose balls, well, that was enough.

S. L. Price

on the 2005 Carolina team

T eamwork was a hard sell for this group. . . . We were selfish. This time around, everyone is losing himself in the team.

Sean May
on the 2005 national champions

❋ ❋ ❋

S ean May embodied the dignified fierceness of a James Worthy or Bobby Jones. Raymond Felton's game-winning steal fit right in with the intensity that caused Chris Webber's 1993 timeout and Fred Brown's 1982 pass and Wilt Chamberlain's bewilderment back in '57: opponents undone, Carolina championships won—with bruising defense, intelligence, and hustle.

S. L. Price
on the 2005 team

❋ ❋ ❋

T his season, something changed. The team closed ranks, adopting an all-business attitude while tuning out all outside opinion and influence. Potential stepped up to meet reality.

Tim Keown
ESPN the Magazine,
on the 2005 Tar Heels

ROYAL COURTS
OF BLUE

T he only sources of heat were potbellied stoves and big wattage bulbs underneath the players' benches. Talk about roughing it; there were no dressing rooms and barely adequate toilet facilities. Players dressed in Emerson Stadium and made the 300-yard trek to the "Tin Can" to practice or play games.

Ken Rappoport

on one of the early Tar Heel venues

T imes were tough in America in the wake of the Depression, and the North Carolina basketball team played in an arena that reflected the era. It was a spare steel structure called the Indoor Athletic Court, nicknamed "The Tin Can."

Ken Rappoport

❀ ❀ ❀

T he Tin Can was always freezing. They had icicles in the corner, I remember.

George Shepard
head coach (1932–35)

❀ ❀ ❀

W e had blankets and wore heavy sweat clothes. Later on they did get central heating in there, but it was never adequate.

George Shepard
on conditions inside the Tin Can

THE ROYAL COURTS OF BLUE

*F*ive different arenas have been called home by the Tar Heels during the team's nearly 100 years of intercollegiate play.

Beginning in 1911, in its first season, Carolina hosted its games in Bynum Gymnasium, ultimately accumulating a 62–11 overall home record through the 1923 season.

From 1924 to '37, the Indoor Athletic Center, better known as the Old Tin Can, housed the Tar Heels, who recorded an impressive 120–18 overall mark during their tenure there. In 1938, the team moved into 4,500-seat Woollen Gym, posting a phenomenal 219–30 record over 28 seasons.

Next came 8,800-capacity Carmichael Auditorium, which opened in December 1965. Carolina won two national championships during its 21 seasons at Carmichael (1957, 1982) en route to an enviable 169–20 record.

The current home of the Heels is the Smith Center, which opened in 1991 and seats 21,572. All the dwellings brought good luck and presented great basketball. At all five venues, Carolina won its inaugural games.

The Tar Heels once enjoyed one of the most formidable home court advantages in all of college basketball. From 1966 to 1986, they played home games at Carmichael Auditorium, which with its metal bleachers, metal roof, and undistinguished exterior looked more like a high school gymnasium than a basketball palace. But somewhere in that venerable building some Tar Heel magic resided. Carolina lost just twenty games in twenty years on that court, and its home-court comebacks became legendary.

Adam Lucas

W e go back and practice there when they're using this [the Smith Center] for concerts. It brings back pleasant memories walking in there. It sure does pale in comparison to size. The noise reverberating, even at a practice session, is remarkable, even the chatter on the court, or me yelling.

Dean Smith
on Carmichael Auditorium

When I give people tickets, I tell them, "You're in the building, but you may not be in Orange County."

Rick Brewer

on seats in the spacious Dean E. Smith Center, which has housed more than 23,000 people for a game

Although the Tar Heels engineered several memorable comebacks in the Smith Center—proving that they had at least as much to do with preparation and talent as with luck—the same magic never surrounded the building. It was enormous, seating 21,750 fans, more than twice Carmichael's capacity. Instead of uncomfortable metal bleachers that practically forced the occupant to stand, the first six rows are made up of cushioned seats that resemble first-class seats on an airplane.

Adam Lucas

T he Dean E. Smith Center is an expansive monument to basketball.

Adam Lucas

WINNING
AND LOSING

W e've learned how fun it is to win. And we've learned how hard it is to win.

Sean May

B ack in 1968, he had decided to never talk to the team about a loss immediately afterwards.

Art Chansky

on a tenet of the Dean Smith philosophy

❀ ❀ ❀

O ur winning streak had to end sometime, and this looks like it. So, fellows, let's lose graciously. When the gun goes off, go right over and congratulate those Maryland boys.

Frank McGuire

to his Tar Heel players during the undefeated, national championship year of 1957, in a game against Maryland, in which North Carolina trailed the Terrapins by six points with a minute to play. McGuire's reverse psychology worked, as UNC came back to notch a 66–61 win in double overtime, extending the Heels' winning streak to 17 games

L earning how to win is playing with poise and making plays regardless of the score or how much pressure somebody may be feeling.

Roy Williams

❋ ❋ ❋

I n twenty-two years of games in Blue Heaven, Smith's teams lost only twenty times, posting six and a half undefeated seasons and staging some of the most memorable victories and comebacks in Carolina history.

Art Chansky

*on Smith's impeccable record
at Carmichael Auditorium*

❋ ❋ ❋

I love being the underdog if we're really good. If we're not any good, I don't like it. It's a great weapon if you can make a team that is really good feel that everyone is against you or they're the underdog.

Roy Williams

M ichael Jordan and Sam Perkins sat stunned in the solemn locker room. Matt Doherty cried so hard in front of the TV cameras that he had hecklers on his answering machine when he returned home. The three had played their last game in a Tar Heel uniform.

Art Chansky

*following North Carolina's 72–68 loss
to Indiana in the 1984 NCAA East Regional
semifinals*

T he most difficult thing about the NCAA Tournament [is] the swiftness and the suddenness and the finality with which it is over.

Roy Williams

HEARTBREAKING END
FOR THE '87 HEELS

One of the toughest losses of Dean Smith's esteemed career at North Carolina came in the 1987 East Regional finals, a 79–75 loss to Syracuse at the Meadowlands.

Smith's decision to play talented guard Jeff Lebo, who only 24 hours earlier had been completely incapacitated by the flu, would be second-guessed. Lebo had difficulty keeping up on both ends of the court.

The loss was felt more deeply than the 1984 defeat to Indiana in the East Regional semifinals, because the '87 group, composed of seniors Kenny Smith, Joe Wolf, Dave Popson, and Curtis Hunter, stormed through their careers, winning 115 games and twice completing the ACC regular season undefeated.

But in the end, the talented 1987 Tar Heels failed to win one ACC Tournament or reach the Final Four.

Some great things happened in the world today. We got Saddam. I'd like to find one of those dad-gum holes he was living in and go there for a little while myself.

Roy Williams

after a disappointingly subpar, ugly win against Akron in his first season as the Tar Heels' coach

When I wasn't able to be emotional on the court, I didn't play well. In games where I was emotional, we won and I played really well. When somebody tries to change the way you've been playing all your life, it's a hard adjustment.

Rashad McCants

on playing for UNC under Matt Doherty

O n March 30, 1991, Dean Smith became the only coach to ever get thrown out of a Final Four game . . . during the Kansas Jayhawks' semifinal win over Carolina. Smith's ejection [came] on his second technical foul in the last minute of play. . . . [He] apologized for "taking the attention away from a great victory for Roy Williams and Kansas."

Art Chansky

I f you guys can't cheer, get your asses to the locker room. . . . If you are very bored, you shouldn't be on our bench.

Roy Williams

chastising Tar Heel players Jesse Holley and Rashad McCants for not cheering after a great defensive effort by an on-court UNC player in a late-December game in 2003 against UNC-Wilmington. Williams sent both to the locker room moments later

Before the 1993 Elite Eight game, [Coach] Smith unwittingly motivated his team against Cincinnati, whose players infuriated the Tar Heels by claiming in print that Smith should have won more than one national championship with all the talent he had had over the years. "Michael Jordan and James Worthy won't be playing for them tomorrow," said Cincy's Nick Van Exel smugly. Derrick Phelps shut down Van Exel in the second half, and Carolina won in overtime 75–68, when Donald Williams drilled two jumpers from three-point land to bury the Bearcats.

Art Chansky

I want my team to want to win. I want them to frickin' make something happen. I get tired of hoping the other team will screw it up.

Roy Williams

❋ ❋ ❋

He hates to lose. In pickup games he would take the worst players and expect to win. Sometimes just by his sheer force of will, he would win games he had no business winning.

Meredith Smith
*Melvin Scott's high school coach,
on Scott*

❋ ❋ ❋

In 1977, Al McGuire's Marquette Warriors shredded the Four Corners to pieces. Every program, like every country, has its Waterloo.

S. L. Price

❋ ❋ ❋

It's been fun to coach to win, instead of to keep from losing.

Dean Smith

T hose guys know what it's like to play at Carolina, the pride it is. To have them still be on our side shows the loyalty that comes with being a part of Carolina basketball.

Jason Capel
*guard/forward (1999–2002),
on the appearance of former Tar Heel players
at a pre-game locker room talk before a
conference game against Florida State,
February 17, 2002, won by North Carolina,
95–85. Up to that point, the Heels had lost
11 of 12 previous games. The former players'
support provided a momentary lift during the
nightmarish 2001–02 season, in which UNC
went 8–20*

I f you think it's OK to lose, that's how you lose thirty-six games in two years. Winning is important. It's not OK to just go through the motions, whether it's a pickup game, pool, or marbles.

Roy Williams

I n college ball, strange things happen. You never know what's going to happen. You just hope that your talent will carry you through.

Bobby Jones
forward (1972–74)

I didn't like that feeling of losing. If we got back, I didn't want to come away with that same feeling, because I felt awful after that.

Jimmy Black
*on losing the NCAA championship game
in 1981 to Indiana, 63–50*

I 'm still not over it. I'm really not. There will be moments when it will pop into my head, maybe when I'm getting ready to close my eyes at night or driving down the highway or on a plane. I don't know if I'll ever get over it. That loss hurts more than any loss I've ever had because we had the best team in the country. We had the best coach in the country. And that's the cruelty of the NCAA Tournament: If it was a best of seven series, we'd have won the national championship, no problem.

Matt Doherty

on his final game as a Tar Heel, the 72–68
loss to Indiana in the second round of the
1984 NCAA Tournament

W inning as a freshman, I didn't have a sense of how important it was, how difficult it was, because we just won right away.

Michael Jordan

* * *

I f we had lost, you would have had so many people knocking the stuffing out of their couches and pillows.

Sam Perkins

on the fortuitous turnout of the 1982 NCAA championship game, won by North Carolina, 63–62

* * *

I t was kind of nerve-wracking, sitting in your room anticipating the game to come. Losing one year [in 1981 against Indiana] and then coming back to win it all was a great accomplishment for us.

Sam Perkins

on the 1982 national champs

C oach Smith seldom talked about winning. Instead he talked about the things we needed to do to be successful. He never got too high after winning or too low after a loss. . . . One of the things I recall best about playing for him came after a heartbreaking loss to Wake Forest in the ACC tournament. He came up to me afterward and thanked me for my effort. That meant a lot to me, to be thanked by my coach after a disappointing loss.

Bobby Jones

I 'll take the losses, you guys take the wins.

Dean Smith
to his teams

W hen Coach Smith went before the reporters after a loss, he put the blame on himself. The players picked up on it, and it took an enormous amount of pressure off our shoulders.

Scott Williams
forward (1987–90)

※ ※ ※

T hey told us they were still with us. But they made it clear they were sick of watching us play the way we were playing.

Jawad Williams
on tough, critical feedback received firsthand by the 2005 Tar Heels, in August 2004, on a surprise campus visit from star alums Vince Carter, Antawn Jamison, Jerry Stackhouse, George Lynch, and Shammond Williams

Nobody said we were going undefeated, but we've got to get it together and stay together.

Sean May

*to his Tar Heel teammates in the locker room
following the 2004–05 season-opening loss
to Santa Clara*

The difference between winning and losing is like this.

Roy Williams

*with his thumb and index finger almost
pinched together*

BITTER FOES

T hough he rarely got caught comparing wins, Dean Smith occasionally admitted that "beating Duke at Duke" ranked among his most favorite moments.

Art Chansky

Although both schools have local rivals that they play every year—UK-Louisville and Carolina-Duke are two of the showcase games in college basketball—fans view the rivalry with the bitterness usually reserved for a neighborhood foe. The two programs have waged a seesaw battle for the title of college basketball's winningest program.

Adam Lucas

on the UNC-Kentucky rivalry

In a way the schools feed off each other, but the nice thing about that rivalry is that I think there's a mutual respect between the coaches and among the players on both teams.

Dean Smith

on the North Carolina-Duke rivalry

I don't know if this old man's heart could have taken it if Danny Ferry had made that one.

Dean Smith

after his team's 77–74 triumph over Duke in 1989. The Blue Devils' Ferry heaved a 75-foot shot at the buzzer that nearly went in

❋ ❋ ❋

In 1995, it was Duke overcoming a 17-point first-half Carolina lead [and Jerry Stackhouse's incredible one-handed reverse thunder-dunk over Eric Meek] at Cameron to build a 12-point second-half advantage. The Tar Heels built an 8-point lead in the first overtime before Jeff Capel hit a running midcourt shot to tie the game and force a second overtime, during which Carolina eventually prevailed, 102–100.

Adam Lucas

O ne hundred and thirty-two straight games [through 2004] have been played in the series with at least one of the two teams ranked.

Adam Lucas

on the phenomenal national level of the Duke-North Carolina rivalry

I was wrong—wrong because we lost. Whether we lose 121–120 or 21–20, we still lost to Duke.

Dean Smith

after North Carolina utilized the stall against Duke in 1965 and lost, 65–62

I wanted to win the game, 2–0. That's just as good as 82–80.

Dean Smith

following Duke's victory in 1979, in which North Carolina held the ball for much of the first half, going scoreless. Duke took a 7–0 lead to the locker room and eventually won, 47–40

T he Demon Deacons . . . are long-standing members of the storied "Big Four" quartet along Tobacco Road, which also includes N.C. State, Duke, and North Carolina. They first met the Tar Heels on the hardwood on February 3, 1911, and have since established one of the longest-running rivalries in the South with the Heels. . . . The teams have met 207 times, a colorful history complete with on-court brawls, shocking upsets, and record-setting individual performances.

Adam Lucas
through 2004

❦ ❦ ❦

W hen you beat Virginia in those days, you more or less had it made.

George Tennent
*Tar Heel basketball letterman from
1916 through '18*

C arolina and Kentucky have a fierce rivalry, which is rare between non-conference foes. Usually it takes close contact for two schools to build hatred, but the Heels and Wildcats have done it while playing just twenty-seven games against each other [through 2005].

Adam Lucas

K entucky coach Adolph Rupp refused to play any games on the North Carolina campus. His explanation was that Carmichael Auditorium did not have a big enough seating capacity. Not that anyone north of Kentucky believed that was the main reason.

Ken Rappoport

This team just had too much fight. . . . Down nine with three minutes to go, I think everybody pretty much thought it was over, but we didn't. I never experienced anything like that, and it's something I'll never forget.

Sean May

on UNC's come-from-behind, 75–73 victory over Duke at Chapel Hill in 2005. In a prodigious performance, May scored 26 points and grabbed 24 rebounds, the most boards by a Carolina player in 37 years

May was fantastic. It was a magnificent individual performance. We lost to a great program with classy kids and a classy coach.

Mike Krzyzewski

after UNC rallied to beat his Blue Devils, 75–73, in 2005 at Chapel Hill

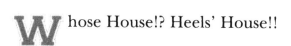

Whose House!? Heels' House!!

Tar Heel players' celebratory
chant
*after beating Duke at Duke, 85–83,
February 1, 2001*

THE TAR HEEL FAITHFUL

I t's tougher on your nerves to be a fan than to be a coach.

Dean Smith

❀ ❀ ❀

F ans claim the Tar Heels never rebuild— they just reload.

John Nichols

P eople who weren't basketball fans suddenly were fans and got really caught up in it. It was like a brushfire across the state.

Woody Durham

on the mania surrounding the 1957 Tar Heels

P ractically everybody left the gym, went out to their cars, started their engines, and put the radios on to listen.

Woody Durham

on the scene at a high school basketball game in 1957 that Durham was attending, when word leaked out that the Tar Heels were in jeopardy of ending their undefeated streak at 16 against Maryland, on February 5, 1957. UNC went on to beat the Terps in double overtime, 65–61

I t was one of the wildest victory celebrations anyone could remember. Some 10,000 fans stormed the Raleigh-Durham airport to welcome home North Carolina's national champions in 1957. Talk about a full-court press.

Ken Rappoport

❋ ❋ ❋

P ete Brennan knew that he and his teammates had done something special when they saw that crowd and when student friends started asking for their autographs.

Ken Rappoport

*on the 1957 NCAA champion Tar Heels' return
to Raleigh-Durham airport following their
triple-overtime win over Kansas to claim
the national crown*

C arolina fans are a "wine-and-cheese crowd."

Sam Cassell

former Florida State guard/
13-year NBA player (through 2006),
during the 1991–92 season

FAST BREAK: *Cassell's remark is in reference to the seating arrangement instituted at the Dean E. Smith Center in 1985, which issued, in essence, a permanent seat license plan placing wealthy season-ticket purchasers courtside, leaving the more raucous and rowdier UNC students away from the action, a consequence that tends to paint Smith Center spectators as staid and too laid-back.*

A t preseason gatherings of the Rams Club, Roy Williams makes a regular part of his stump speech a challenge to season ticket holders to "take off their corporate hats" and come to the games ready to make some noise.

Adam Lucas

Paul and Judy Singleterry live in Mulvane, Kansas, a small community just outside of Wichita. They are attending the midnight practice at Chapel Hill for the third straight year, a feat made even more impressive by the fact that they drive from Kansas to North Carolina for the event.

Adam Lucas

※ ※ ※

It reminds me of the old days, when the Carolina players were like rock stars. Everyone wanted a piece of them.

Woody Durham

on UNC's trip to Boone, North Carolina, in November 2000, to play tiny Appalachian State. The Heels, winners by 30 points, were treated like gods by the local citizenry before and after the game

I didn't realize what we had accomplished until we got back and saw the state that the people of North Carolina and Chapel Hill were in.

Sam Perkins

in the wake of the Tar Heels' 63–62 victory over Georgetown in New Orleans to capture the 1982 NCAA title

⚾ ⚾ ⚾

The popular North Carolina slogan for years was "Duke is puke, Wake is fake, but the team I hate is N.C. State."

Steve Holstrom

E ven now, I get together with other Tar Heel friends to watch basketball games and cheer like when we were 19 years old. The feeling of "Carolina" goes on and on for me and has gotten stronger over the years.

Charlie Burns
Tar Heel player from 1960 through '63

I don't know how many students I've had in here with a textbook in one hand and a tall beer in the other.

Michael Hayek
Chapel Hill, N.C., restaurant general manager, on students waiting inside and outside his establishment since 11 a.m. the day of the 2005 NCAA finals to watch that evening's championship game against Illinois

I think that, after that long, people become more fanatical about it. The Holy Grail of winning it all means a lot more to you than if you win it every couple of years.

Robbie Brafford

UNC graduate,
on the wait for another North Carolina
national championship, on the night of the
2005 NCAA title game against Illinois.
Brafford was a sophomore at UNC in 1993,
when the Tar Heels had last won the national
championship

As a senior officer, I apply the can-do, winning attitude each and every day in my military career. I can only hope that some day the military could have as much pride as UNC basketball has.

James Hamilton

Virginia Beach, Virginia, naval officer

THE
BALL BAG

I'll remember the hugs [from the players] long after I've forgotten cutting down the net.

Roy Williams

I had a coach for four years, but I got a friend for life.

Phil Ford
on Dean Smith

A re you kidding? And miss another year of playing for Dean Smith and Bill Guthridge?

Scott Montross
father of center Eric Montross,
when asked if his son was considering
turning pro after winning the national title
with UNC in 1993

Most of the little guys want to be bigger, but I remember Walter Davis had grown at our place, and got up to six feet, six inches, and he still wanted to be listed as six feet, five inches. I asked him why, and he said, "They'll think I'm a good jumper."

Dean Smith

Republicans buy shoes, too.

Michael Jordan

on criticism for his failure to back a black senatorial candidate in North Carolina who twice ran unsuccessfully against Republican incumbent Jesse Helms. The reference is to his famous line of Nike Air Jordans

I never read the articles about me when I was playing. I just cut them out and put them away. Then one day I started reminiscing, and I went through all the clippings and I said, "Oh, my God, did I do that?"

George Glamack

*North Carolina's famed "Blind Bomber,"
who averaged 20.6 points a game his senior
season of 1941 in an era when teams barely
scored 60 points per contest. Glamack earned
All-America recognition in both 1940 and '41
and was named Helms Foundation National
Player of the Year both years*

O ne, two, three, 30!

Tar Heel players' chant
*on the first day of practice before the
1981–82 season. The 30 signifies the 30th
day of the third month of the year—the day
after the NCAA finals: a day in which the
players hoped to wake up happy following a
championship game victory*

❀ ❀ ❀

B y the time we had got back in there, we whooped and hollered for about two more minutes, and then, it was just silent. I started crying. I was looking throughout the room, and just looking at their faces, seeing how happy they were, and what it meant to them.

Jim Braddock
*in the locker room immediately following the
team's 63–62 victory over Georgetown for the
1982 NCAA championship*

W hen I was going to school, looking back on it now, it was never considered a big deal that we had never won a national championship. It was really something the media picked up on. Even if they had not won that thing in '82, it's still the best basketball program in America.

Mitch Kupchak

I think, overall, that's when everyone's awareness of the school magnified, doubled. Including mine. That's when I saw the system on a level that hadn't been played before and that's when I became interested in going to the school.

Kenny Smith
*on his perception of UNC after the 1982
NCAA championship game win*

Picking second and needing a point guard, the Atlanta Hawks grab [small forward] Marvin Williams. . . . To sum up his UPPPPPPPPside as an NBA prospect, [analyst] Jay Bilas uses phrases like, "Sky is the limit . . . unbelievably long . . . active, athletic . . . the real deal . . . the complete package . . . active, bouncy, athlete . . . really long . . . wingspan of about seven foot three . . . " and then adds, "The thing that makes him special is his range as a shooter." [Of course, nowhere in that gushing monologue was the phrase, "Couldn't start for his college team." But we'll let it slide. I like Jay Bilas. He's unbelievably long.]

Bill Simmons
"Page Two," ESPN.com

O f course, we thought we had David all along. He had been a Carolina fan.

Dean Smith

on college legend David Thompson, who went on to star at N.C. State in the mid-1970s

C harlotte Bobcats. Bernie Bickerstaff and company picked two winners in Raymond Felton and Sean May. The two Tar Heels were national champions and they join another player who cut down the net in college in Emeka Okafor. Felton and May will help put people in the seats, too. I give them an A+.

Dick Vitale

*"Post-draft thoughts: Wild night,"
Special to ESPN.com*

SEAN MAY? SEAN WILL!
RASHAD McCANTS? RASHAD McCAN!

Placards seen behind the
North Carolina bench

*during UNC's 2005 Final Four victory
over Michigan State*

❋ ❋ ❋

He's been living in my dad's footsteps. Now he's got a championship ring of his own. He deserves it.

Scott May Jr.

*Sean's older brother, a walk-on on Indiana's
2002 national runner-up team*

❋ ❋ ❋

You guys almost gave me a heart attack, but you got it done.

Michael Jordan

*to the 2005 national champion Tar Heels
following their 75–70 NCAA finals win
over Illinois*

We're still the playground kings of yesterday.

James Worthy

NORTH CAROLINA NATIONAL CHAMPION ROSTERS

*I*n the five national championship seasons in Chapel Hill, many a Tar Heel has played the role of small cog in the big wheel. The following roster listings are a salute to all the players— stars and supporting cast—who have helped spell the ultimate in success for North Carolina basketball.

1923–24
26–0
(National champions in Helms Foundation poll)
Norman Shepard, coach

Cartwright Carmichael

Jack Cobb

Billy Devin

Bill Dodderer

Donald Koonce

Henry Lineberger

Sam "Monk" McDonald

Jimmy Poole

Starters in bold

1956–57
32–0
(NCAA national champions)
Frank McGuire, coach

No.		Pos	Hgt	Wgt	Class
10	**Lennie Rosenbluth**	F	6–5	195	Sr
35	**Pete Brennan**	F	6–6	190	Jr
33	Danny Lotz	F	6–7	198	So
22	Roy Searcy	F	6–4	185	Jr
31	Gehrmann Holland	F	6–3	200	So
41	**Joe Quigg**	C	6–9	205	Jr
30	Bill Hathaway	C	6–11	240	So
40	**Tommy Kearns**	G	5–11	188	Jr
44	Tony Radovich	G	6–2	192	Sr
32	**Bob Cunningham**	G	6–4	190	Jr
43	Stan Groll	G	6–0	182	So
11	Ken Rosemond	G	5–8	150	Jr

1981–82
32–2
(NCAA national champions)
Dean Smith, coach

No.		Pos	Hgt	Wgt	Class
4	Lynwood Robinson	G	6–1	176	Fr
21	**Jimmy Black**	G	6–3	162	Sr
22	Buzz Peterson	G	6–3½	165	Fr
23	**Mike Jordan**	G/F	6–5	189	Fr
24	Jim Braddock	G	6–2	171	Jr
32	John Brownlee	F/C	6–10	215	Fr
33	Dean Shaffer	G	6–4	194	So
41	**Sam Perkins**	C	6–9	224	So
43	Jeb Barlow	F	6–8	207	Sr
44	**Matt Doherty**	F	6–8	210	So
45	Chris Brust	F	6–9	231	Sr
50	Cecil Exum	F	6–6	206	So
51	Timo Makkonen	C	6–11½	202	So
52	**James Worthy**	F	6–9	219	Jr
54	Warren Martin	F/C	6–11	222	Fr

1992–93
34–4
(NCAA national champions)
Dean Smith, coach

No.		Pos	Hgt	Wgt	Class
24	Dante Calabria	G	6–4	186	Fr
11	Scott Cherry	G	6–5	180	Sr
4	Larry Davis	G	6–3	184	Fr
40	Ed Geth	F	6–9	250	Fr
34	**George Lynch**	F	6–8	220	Sr
00	**Eric Montross**	C	7–0	270	Jr
14	**Derrick Phelps**	G	6–3	181	Jr
31	**Brian Reese**	F	6–6	215	Jr
5	Henrik Rodl	G	6–8	203	Sr
33	Kevin Salvadori	C/F	7–0	224	Jr
35	Travis Stephenson	F	6–7	222	Sr
3	Pat Sullivan	F	6–8	216	Jr
55	Matt Wenstrom	C	7–1	260	Sr
21	**Donald Williams**	G	6–3	194	So
45	Serge Zwikker	C	7–3	248	Fr

2004–05
33–4
(NCAA national champions)
Roy Williams, coach

No.		Pos	Hgt	Wgt	Class
15	Charlie Everett	F	6–3	210	Sr
2	**Raymond Felton**	G	6–1	198	Jr
4	Brooks Foster	G	6–2	190	Fr
25	Damion Grant	C	6–11	260	Jr
0	Jesse Holley	G	6–3	190	So
35	C. J. Hooker	F	6–2	188	Sr
5	**Jackie Manuel**	G/F	6–5	192	Sr
42	**Sean May**	F/C	6–9	260	Jr
32	**Rashad McCants**	F/G	6–4	207	Jr
22	Wes Miller	G	5–11	185	So
34	David Noel	F	6–6	230	Jr
41	Byron Sanders	F	6–9	230	Jr
1	Melvin Scott	G	6–2	190	Sr
3	Reyshawn Terry	F	6–8	214	So
11	Quentin Thomas	G	6–3	185	Fr
21	**Jawad Williams**	F	6–9	220	Sr
24	Marvin Williams	F	6–9	230	Fr

BIBLIOGRAPHY

Alexander, Chip and Dane Hoffman. *Tar Heel Trivia: Tantalizing Tidbits from a Basketball Powerhouse.* Chapel Hill, N.C.: Village Sports, 1991.

Bergeron, Elena. "NCAA Tourney '05: Guard Dogs: Trespass on their turf and they will bite back." *ESPN the Magazine*, March 28, 2005: 76.

Bowers, Matt, ed. *Carolina: 2004-05 Tar Heels Basketball.* Chapel Hill, N.C.: UNC Athletic Communications Office, 2004.

Browning, Wilt. "Horace A. "Bones" McKinney." *The North Carolina Century: Tar Heels Who Made a Difference, 1900-2000.* Eds. Howard E. Covington Jr. and Marion A. Ellis. Charlotte, N.C.: Levine Museum of the New South, 2002: 608-609.

Carey, Jack. "N. Carolina shows grit in win." *USA Today*, March 7, 2005: 7C

Chansky, Art. *Dean's Domain: The Inside Story of Dean Smith and His College Basketball Empire.* Marietta, Ga.: Longstreet, Inc., 1999.

Chansky, Art. *The Dean's List: A Celebration of Tar Heel Basketball and Dean Smith.* New York: Warner Books, Inc., 1996.

Daly, David. *One to Remember: The 1982 North Carolina Tar Heels NCAA Championship Team, Then and Now.* Asheboro, N.C.: Down Home Press, 1991.

Darcy, Kieran. "NCAA Tourney '05: The Beasts Within: These terrorizing bigs put on a horror show down low." *ESPN the Magazine*, March 28, 2005: 74.

DeWitt, David. *True Blue: Matt Doherty Returns to Carolina Basketball.* Lanham, Md.: Diamond Communications, 2002.

Gustafson, John. "NCAA Tourney '05: Improv Artists: When the ball is in their hands, keep an eye on it—if you can." *ESPN the Magazine*, March 28, 2005: 73.

Holstrom, Steve. *The Carolina Corporation: Inside Dean Smith and the Tar Heels.* Dallas, Texas: Taylor Publishing Company, 1988.

Jacobs, Barry. *The World According to Dean: Four Decades of Basketball as Seen by Dean Smith.* New York: Total Sports, Inc., 1998.

Jacobs, Barry. *Three Paths to Glory: A Season on the Hardwood with Duke, N.C. State, and North Carolina.* New York: Macmillan Publishing Company, 1993.

Keown, Tim. "...The Time Is Now." *ESPN the Magazine*, March 28, 2005: 68, 70.

Kilgo, John. "Dean Smith." *The North Carolina Century: Tar Heels Who Made a Difference, 1900-2000.* Eds. Howard E. Covington Jr. and Marion A. Ellis. Charlotte, N.C.: Levine Museum of the New South, 2002: 615-616.

Lawrence, Andrew. "The NCAAs, Rounds 1 & 2: Rising to the Challenge." *Sports Illustrated Presents: A Special Collector's Edition: North Carolina Tar Heels, National Champions 2005*: 51, 53.

Lucas, Adam. *Going Home Again: Roy Williams, the North Carolina Tar Heels, and a Season to Remember.* Guilford, Conn.: The Lyons Press, 2004.

Morrill, Julia. "The NCAAs, Rounds 3 & 4: The Wake-Up Call." *Sports Illustrated Presents: A Special Collector's Edition: North Carolina Tar Heels, National Champions 2005*: 56-57.

Nichols, John. *Tobacco Road!: The North Carolina*

Tar Heels Story. Mankato, Minn.: Creative Education, 2000.

Patterson, Donald W. "Michael J. Jordan." *The North Carolina Century: Tar Heels Who Made a Difference, 1900-2000.* Eds. Howard E. Covington Jr. and Marion A. Ellis. Charlotte, N.C.: Levine Museum of the New South, 2002: 600-603.

Price, S.L. "The Carolina Standard." *Sports Illustrated Presents: A Special Collector's Edition: North Carolina Tar Heels, National Champions 2005*: 12-13.

Rappoport, Ken. *Tales from the Tar Heel Locker Room: A Collection of the Greatest Tar Heel Stories Ever Told!* Sports Publishing L.L.C., 2002.

Scott, David. *Quotable Dean Smith: Words of Insight, Inspiration, and Intense Preparation by and about Dean Smith, the Dean of College Basketball Coaches.* Hendersonville, Tenn.: TowleHouse Publishing, 2004.

Shanken, Marvin R. "One-on-One with Michael Jordan." *Cigar Aficionado,* August 2005: 70-72.

Smith, Dean and Gerald D. Bell with John Kilgo. *The Carolina Way: Leadership Lessons from a Life in Coaching.* New York: The Penguin Press, 2004.

Syken, Bill, compiled by. "The Season in Pictures: Great Leap Forward." *Sports Illustrated Presents: A Special Collector's Edition: North Carolina Tar Heels, National Champions 2005*: 34.

Vitale, Dick. "NCAA Tourney '05: Count It." *ESPN the Magazine,* March 28, 2005: 81.

Wahl, Grant. "Return of the Native." *Sports Illustrated Presents: A Special Collector's Edition: North Carolina Tar Heels, National Champions 2005*: 27-28.

Wahl, Grant. "The Tao of Rashad." *Sports Illustrated Presents: A Special Collector's Edition: North Carolina Tar Heels, National Champions 2005*: 17, 19, 21.

Williamson, Thad. *More Than a Game: Why North*

Carolina Basketball Means So Much to So Many. Cambridge, Mass.: Economic Affairs Bureau, 2001.

Wolff, Alexander. "The NCAAs, The Final Four: Above Them All." *Sports Illustrated Presents: A Special Collector's Edition: North Carolina Tar Heels, National Champions 2005*: 60, 65.

WEB SITES:

Associated Press. "Tar Heels coach closer to elusive title." ESPN.com. http://sports.espn.go.com/ncb/recap?gameId=254000062, April 2, 2005.

Beard, Aaron. "45,000 Tar Heels fans flock to Franklin Street in peace." Associated Press. http://www.usatoday.com/sports/college/mensbasketball/tourney05/2005-04-05-unc-fans_x.htm, April 5, 2005.

Forde, Pat. "UNC comes together a team, exits as champs." ESPN.com. http://sports.espn.go.com/ncb/ncaatourney05/news/story?id=2011555, April 4, 2005.

Lopresti, Mike. "UNC conquers Michigan State, will face Illinois." Gannett News Service. http://usatoday.com/sports/college/mensbasketball/tourney05/2005-04-02-unc-michstate_x.htm, April 3, 2005.

Lucas, Adam. "There's No Slowing Down Hubert Davis: Former Tar Heel star back in town for his annual summer camp." TarHeelBlue.com. http://tarheelblue.collegesports.com/sports/mbaskbl/specrel/062102aaa.html, June 21, 2002.

Simmons, Bill. "A Diary with Upside." ESPN.com. http://sports.espn.go.com/espn/page2/story?page=simmons/050629&num=2, and http://sports.espn.go.com/espn/page2/story?page=simmons/050629&num=3, June 29, 2005.

Vitale, Dick. "Post-draft thoughts: Wild night." Special to ESPN.com. http://espn.go.com/dickvitale/vcolumn050628-NBA-postdraft.html, June 28, 2005

INDEX